BLACKBURN

From Old Photographs

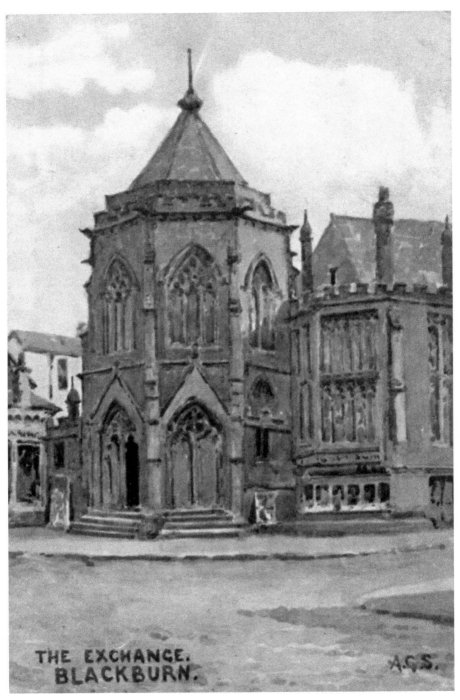

THE EXCHANGE.
BLACKBURN.

A.G.S.

The Exchange, Blackburn, *c.* 1910. This and the next three illustrations are taken from a series of paintings of Blackburn by A.G. Stewart published as postcards by J.W. Ruddock of Lincoln in their 'Artists Series' in about 1910.

BLACKBURN

From Old Photographs

RAY B. SMITH

AMBERLEY

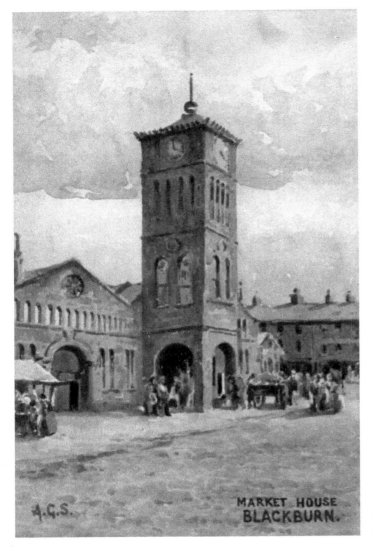

Market House, Blackburn,
c. 1910.

This edition first publishied 2010

Amberley Publishing Plc
Cirencester Road, Chalford,
Stroud, Gloucestershire, GL6 8PE

www.amberley-books.com

Copyright © Ray B. Smith, 2010

The right of Ray B. Smith to be identified as the Author
of this work has been asserted in accordance with the
Copyrights, Designs and Patents Act 1988.

ISBN 978 1 84868 144 6

British Library Cataloguing in Publication Data.
A catalogue record for this book is available from the
British Library.

Typesetting and Origination by Fonthill.
Printed in Great Britain.

Contents

Introduction   7

1. News   9

2. Street Scenes   17

3. Commerce   49

4. People   59

5. Church and Education   71

6. Leisure   91

7. Transport   111

8. The Lighter Side   119

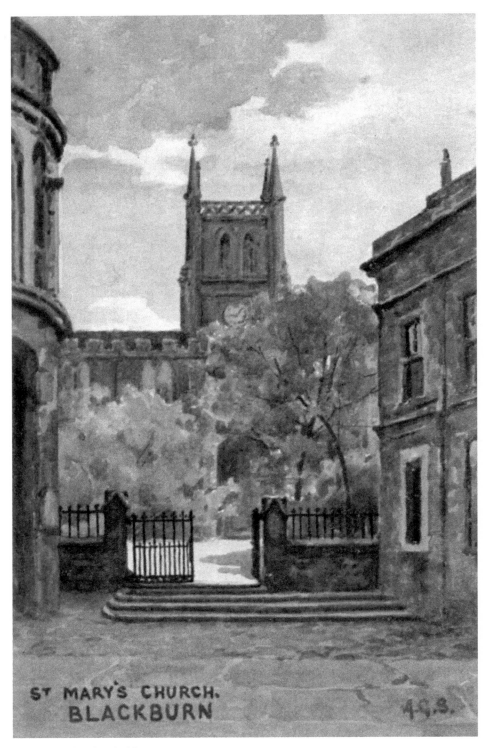

St Mary's Church, Blackburn, *c.* 1910.

Introduction

This book is not intended as a history of Blackburn but more of a collection of interesting pictures of everyday life over the years which include people as well as buildings. The majority of the photographs are from postcards which deal with a period from 1900 to the 1930s. These I have been collecting for many years trying to put together all the sets that were ever published including those being printed today. My interest in Blackburn's history has also led to me collecting crested china, books, pamphlets, photographs, letter heads, newspapers, in fact anything to do with old Blackburn, up to the great demolition period of the 1960s.

As well as old postcard images I have been fortunate to be able to include many press photographs from the archives of the late Wally Talbot by kind permission of his son Howard. Those chosen for inclusion here are from the 1950s and 60s and will be of particular interest to readers who will remember this period better than the pre-war years which are represented mainly by the postcard images.

When I was originally approached, the opportunity satisfied my ambition to publish a book of Blackburn using as many pictures as possible that had not been seen before in print. Some of the pictures in my own collection have, in fact, already appeared in other books so in order to balance the content of the book I have included a few which have been previously seen and I have drawn on the collections of others when necessary. I wish to thank particularly, in this context, David Frankland and Steve Owens for their interest and support and Alvin Cook, John Clough and Jim Marginson for adding the final touches.

I have made the captions as informative as possible but if readers have more information or knowledge about any of them I would be very pleased to receive it.

Ray B. Smith
Blackburn

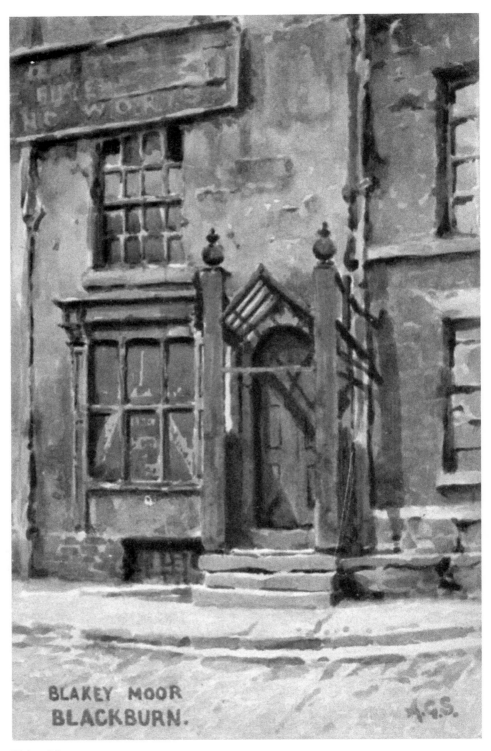

Blakey Moor, *c.* 1910.

one

News

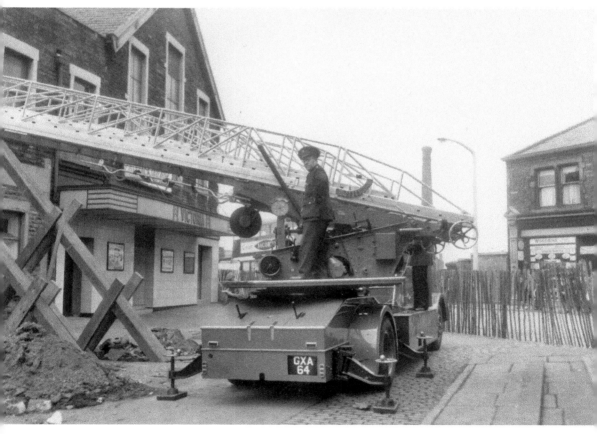

The Victoria Picture Hall on Higher Bam Street, Higher Eanam, collapsed in April 1960 and ultimately had to be demolished. It had been built in 1908 but was not as famous as its counterpart, the Alexandra Picture Palace or 'Penks' as it was commonly known, across the road in Dock Street.

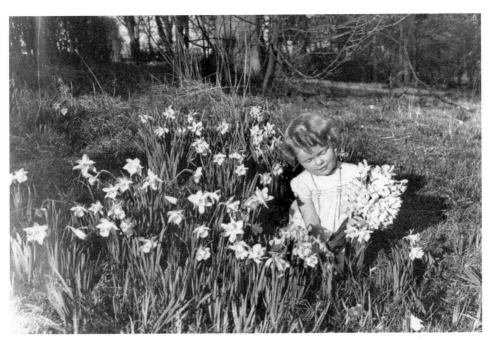

Do you remember picking daffodils in Woodfold Park in 1956 when this picture was taken?

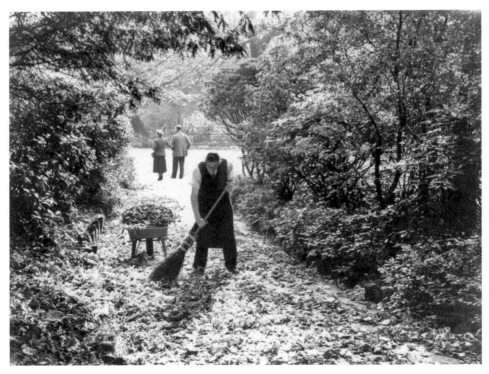

Autumn in Corporation Park in 1956. The park keeper today has mechanical means of collecting up the leaves.

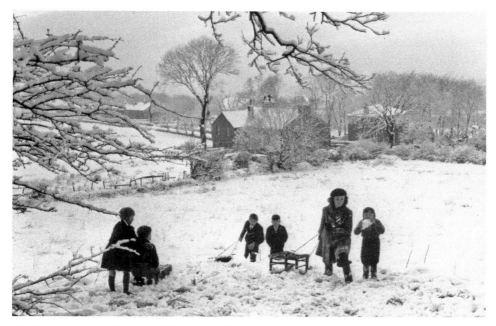

Sledging behind the Clog and Billycock on Friesland in 1959.

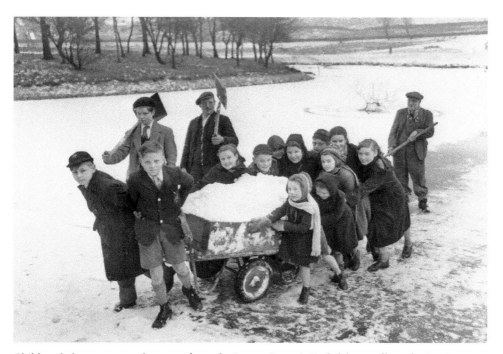

Children help to remove the snow from the ice on Queen's Park lake to allow skating in 1959. This was a regular sport in the winters up to the 1960s before the weather seemed to get milder. The water level in the lake was deliberately allowed to fall before freezing over to improve safety for the skaters.

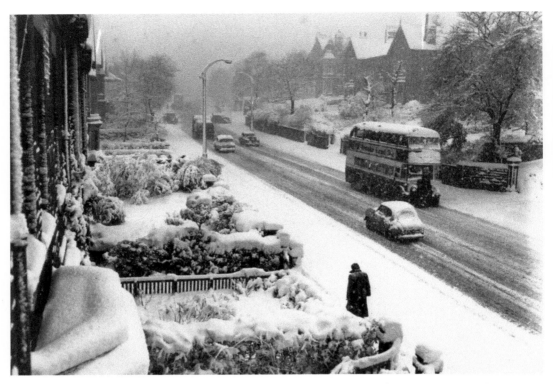

This was what it was like going to school or work down Preston New Road on a winter's morning in 1956. Adelaide Terrace can be seen in the middle top of the picture.

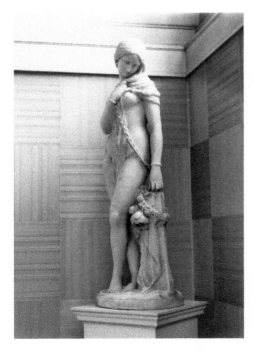

A statue called the Octoroon on the staircase of the Old Town Hall photographed in May 1962. The story goes that one mayor took exception to the nudity of the two statues on the stairs and ordered them to be covered up while he was mayor.

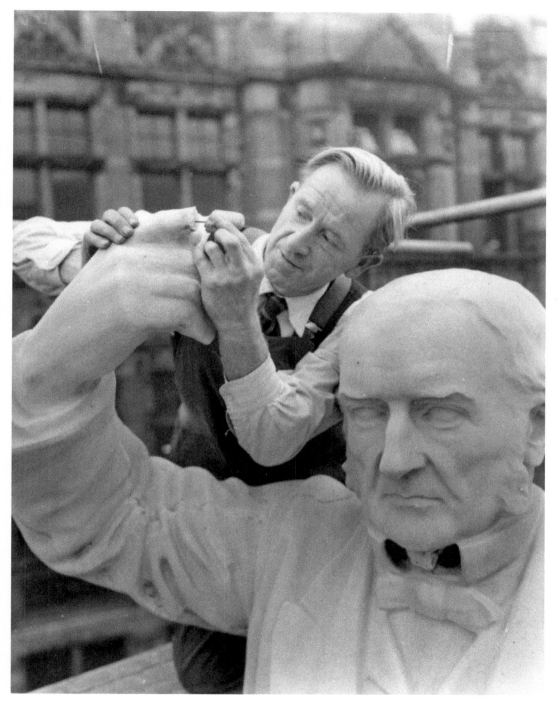

Mr Cookson of Cookson Bros, opposite the cemetery, repairs the finger on Gladstone's statue in October 1956. It had been damaged in the 'flitting' from the Boulevard to Blakey Moor.

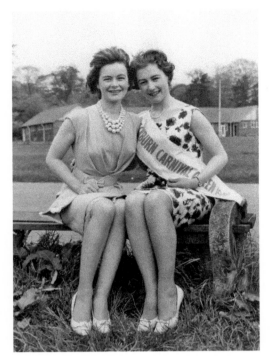

Carnival Queen Raye Williams with Sabina
Smith in June 1961.

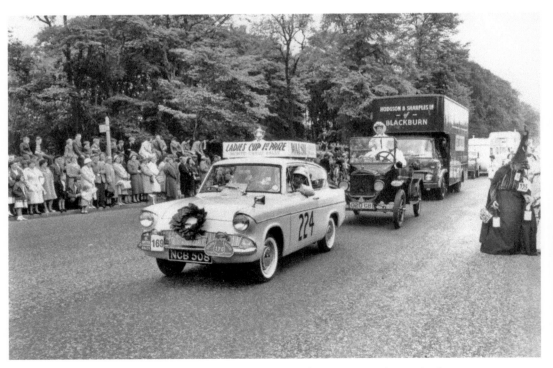

The procession of floats to the Carnival at Witton Park which was an annual event in the 1960s.

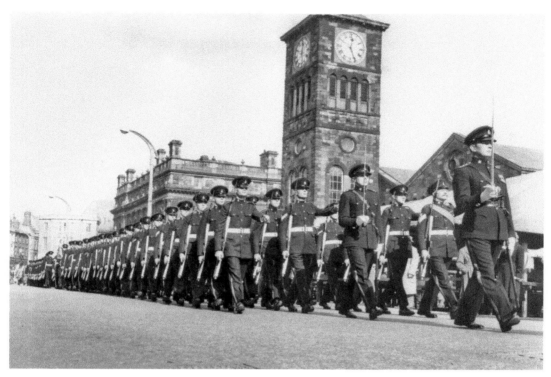

The East Lancashire Regiment was given the freedom of the Borough of Blackburn on 17 April 1948 which allowed them to parade once a year through the Borough with drums beating, bands playing, colours flying and with bayonets fixed. The Prince of Wales Volunteers of the Lancashire Regiment did just that in September 1960.

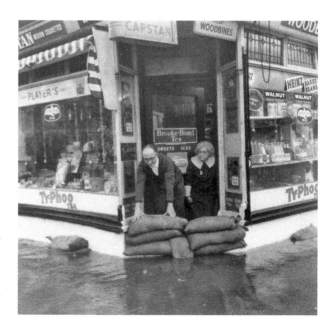

The corner shop at 336 Whalley New Road, on the corner of Agate Street, was marooned in December 1964. Flooding was a regular occurrence in the Roe Lee and cemetery areas prior to new sewers being laid later.

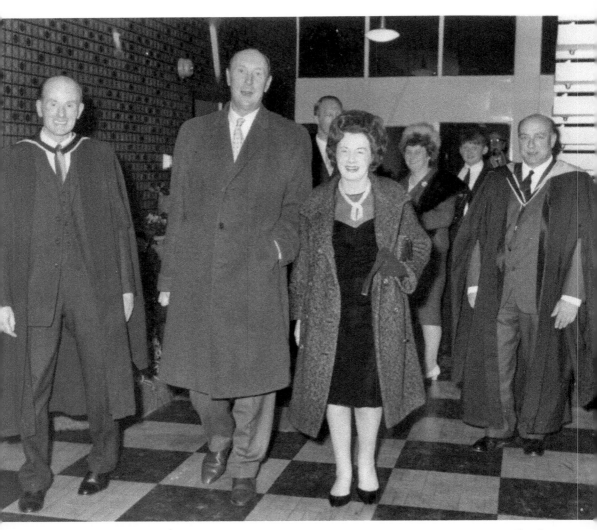

Barbara Castle MP accompanies Chief Constable Bibby and Mr Griffin (headmaster), at the official opening of Billinge Grammar School at Troy in March 1966.

two

Streets and Buildings

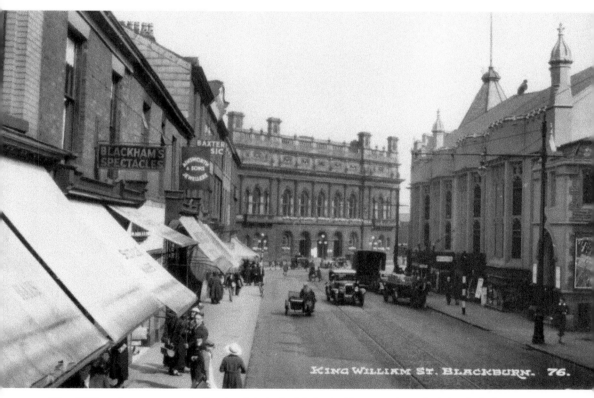

King William Street, pre-1938. On the right is the Majestic Cinema and on the left, Blackahm &
Co., opticians, Ainsworth & Sons, jewellers, and H.L. Baxter Ltd, booksellers – who also had a
lending library. Further down were Mabel Stevenson's and Nottingham House. The Majestic was
showing the film *13 Hours by Air* starring Fred MacMurray and Joan Bennett.

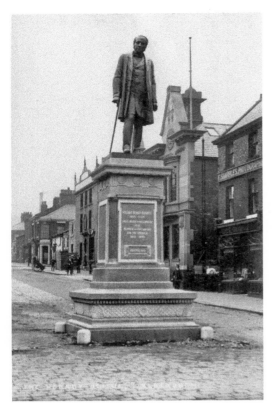

The Hornby Statue, which cost in the region of £3,000, in its original position at the bottom of Limbrick. To the right is the studio of the well-known photographer Frederick W.E. Sharples, next to which is the YMCA – now the Elma Yerburgh pub. The next two blocks above have been demolished for Barbara Castle Way. The Sir Charles Napier pub can be seen behind the statue. The corner shop on Kirkham Lane was a hairdressers before becoming a confectioners. Behind the shop, during the last war, Peggy Wilson held her dancing school. The statue, erected in 1912, is inscribed 'William Henry Hornby, 1805-1894, first mayor of Blackburn 1851, Member of Parliament for the Borough 1857-1869'.

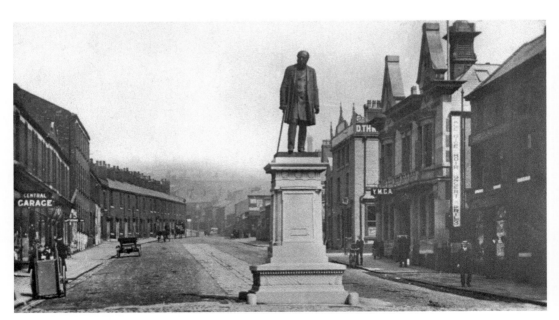

Another wider view of Limbrick in 1928 showing Walsh's Ford, car dealers, on the left with a Ford Model T outside, and, further up, a Brook Bond Tea van.

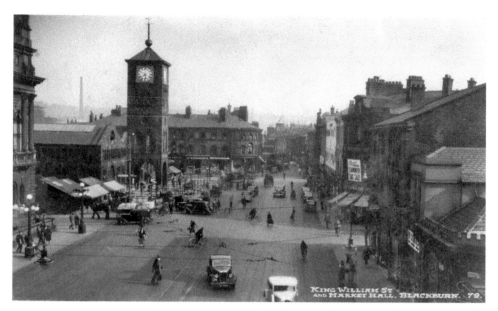

This pre-1938 view further down King William Street, at the front of the town hall, shows the market hall and the skeletons of stalls for market day. On the front right is Singer's sewing machine shop and Ellwoods are having a summer sale. Facing in the background are the Victoria Buildings where George W. Ainsworth, goldsmith, was situated and to the right, J. Hargreaves & Sons, tobacconists.

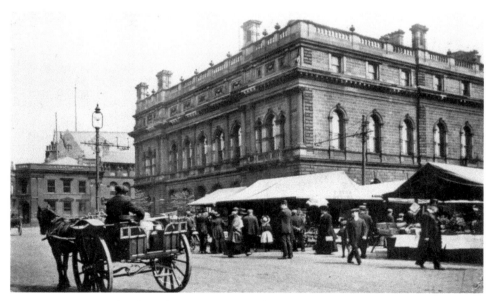

A 1916 scene on market day. The traditional milk float in the foreground from which milk was dispersed by measures into jugs which were then covered with a net with beads around the edge to hold it on.

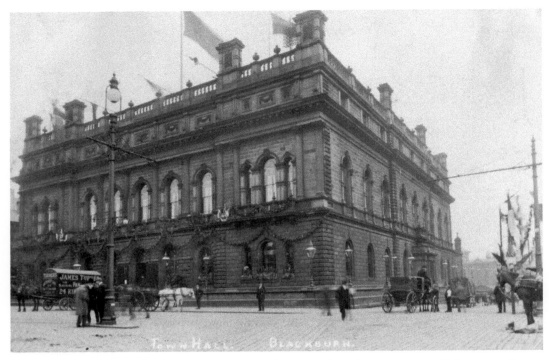

The Town Hall decorated for the visit of Princess Louise on 30 September 1905 to unveil the statue of Queen Victoria on the boulevard (see photograph below). Note the James Turner furniture wagon and several other types of horse-drawn transport.

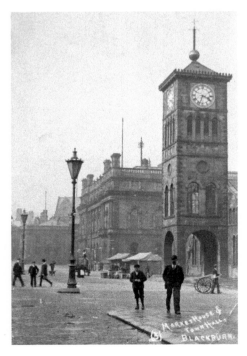

Another view of the Town Hall of 1907 showing a few market stalls and activity either after the market or before.

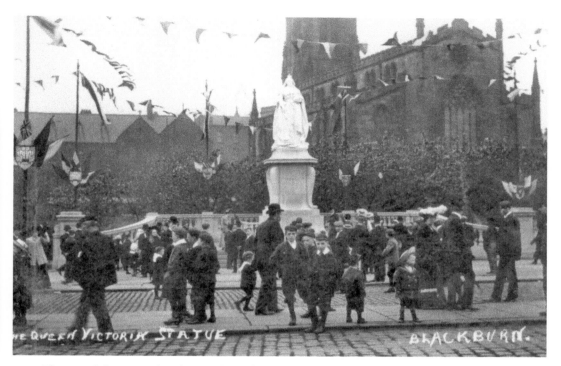

The crowd disperses after the unveiling of the statue. Note the interesting garb of the children of the period.

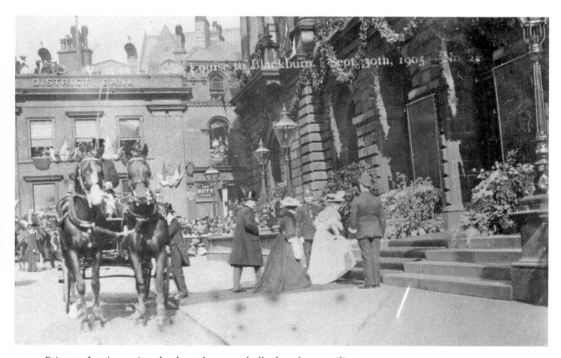

Princess Louise arrives back at the town hall after the unveiling.

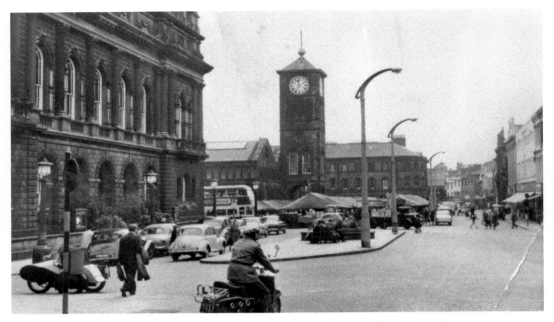

A 1960s view of King William Street with more modern transport than we have seen so far in previous pictures, including the mayor's car. No such thing as one-way streets yet.

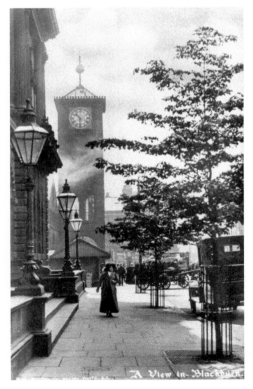

A lovely view from the front of the Town Hall just prior to the First World War. Looks like the ball above the clock tower has stuck, as it was raised at noon and dropped at 1 o'clock when the gun was fired.

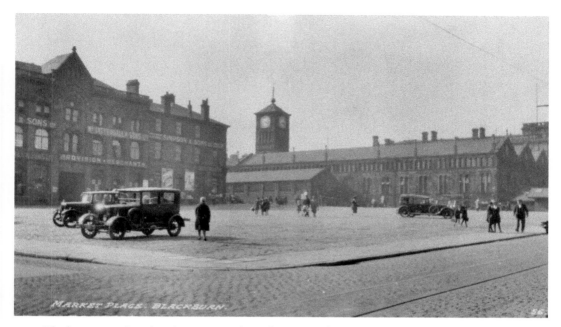

The bottom market place in 1938 seen from the corner of Victoria Street and Lord Street. Rakestraw's carpet warehouse is on the left (see p. 49) followed by William Tattersall's provision merchants and Simpson & Sons, also provision merchants. The large door in the centre was the entrance to a store for the market stalls.

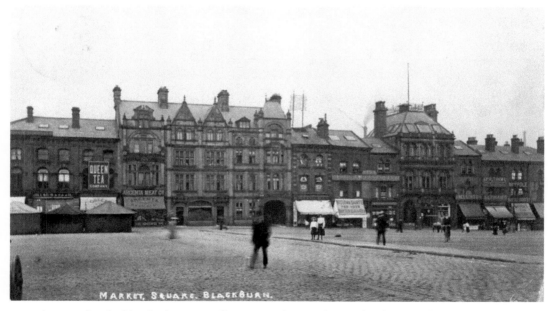

A 1907 view looking in the reverse direction to the one above taken by J.W. Shaw. From left to right: Hill's Bazaar; Queen Tea Co., Argenta Meat Co., The Crown Hotel, W. Hayhurst Ltd, Keeloma Dairy Co., with the Meliora Restaurant above, the Reform Club, B. Brown & Son Ltd, Nelsons, A. Altham Ltd and Maypole Dairy. Hill's Bazaar was later taken over by Marks & Spencer.

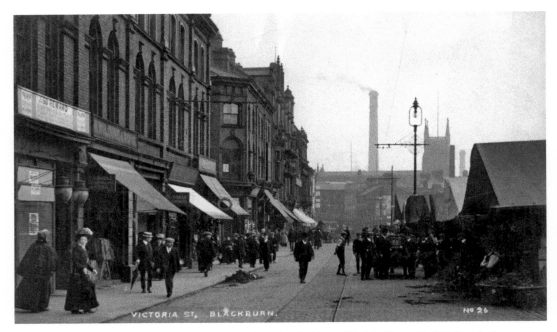

A closer view of Victoria Street in 1913. From the left: Blackburn Weekly News, R. Wilding & Sons; J. Eatough, C. Dean, optician, S. Hilton & Son, boot dealers, followed by Cort Street. The wholesale market stalls are opposite.

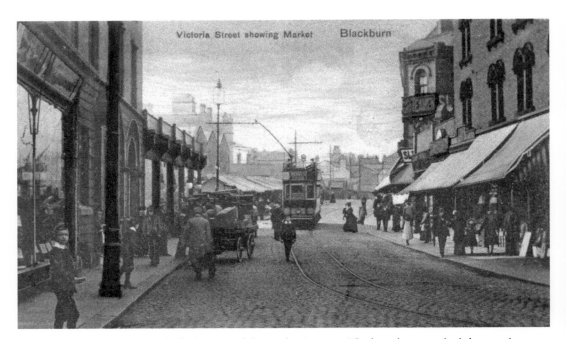

Victoria Street looking towards the bottom of the market in 1906. The low shops on the left were the premises of Johnny Forbes the well known sports outfitters. The first shop on the left is Beatty Bros, tailors, followed by the New Inn public house.

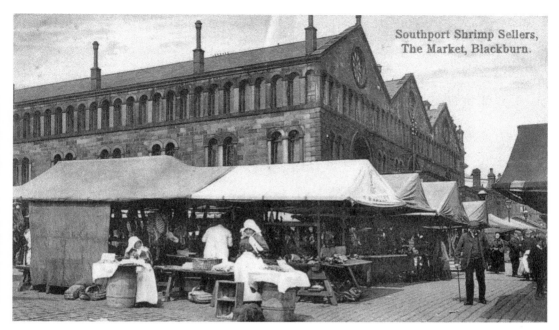

Southport Shrimp Sellers,
The Market, Blackburn.

These shrimp ladies from Southport are seen in an alley off Victoria Street which was just behind the view below which is on Victoria Street itself. There were shrimp ladies here up to the time that the market was closed in the 1960s. The first stall is that of William Hartley.

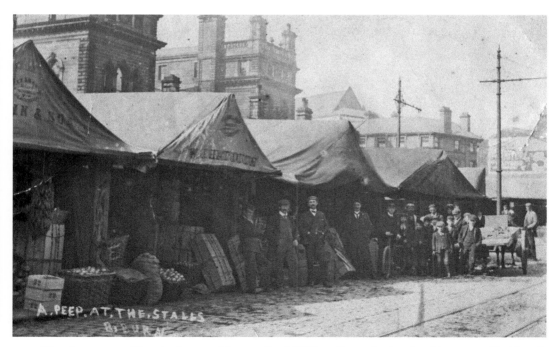

A. PEEP. AT. THE. STALLS.

The frontage to Victoria Street with a stall of William Eatough showing his wares. Blackburn's wholesale fruit and vegetable market was one of the biggest and best in the North West.

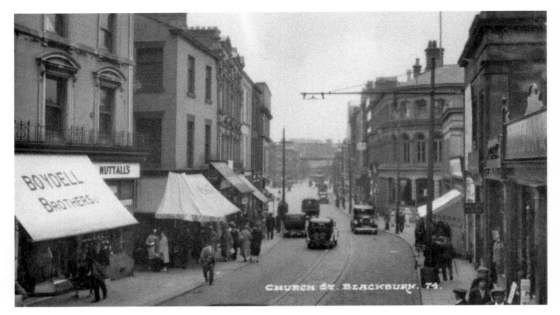

Church Street in 1937, just below Thwaites' Arcade. On the left are Boydell Bros, tailors, Nuttall's Breweries, Shorrock Fold (a passageway to the market), Clifton's confectioners. On the right are Addison's wine merchants and Mason's drapers.

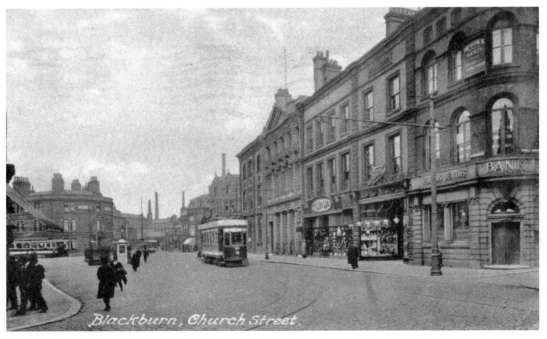

In this view, of 1928, further down, nearing Salford, is William Deacon's Bank, Boots Cash Chemists; A. Tyler & Sons, boot dealers, London City and Midland Bank and The White Bull Hotel. Notice the white telephone kiosk outside the underground toilets.

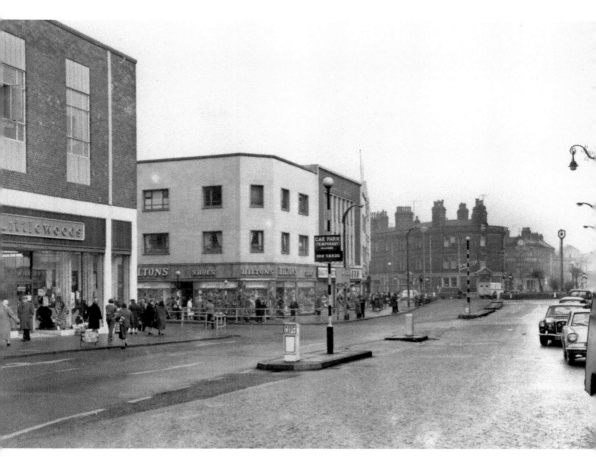

A more up to date scene in Church Street taken in December 1962 showing Littlewoods that had been built on the corner of Victoria Street. Hilton's shoe shop had been redeveloped and the Golden Lion Hotel had been replaced with the Arndale Centre next to Woolworths. The central islands were not a barrier as they are today.

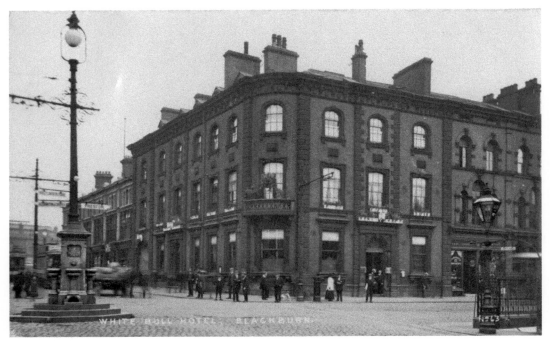

A closer view of the White Bull Hotel in 1905 by A. E. Shaw. The remains of the fountain and lamp standard on the left can still be seen down Pleasington Playing Fields, but without the standard.

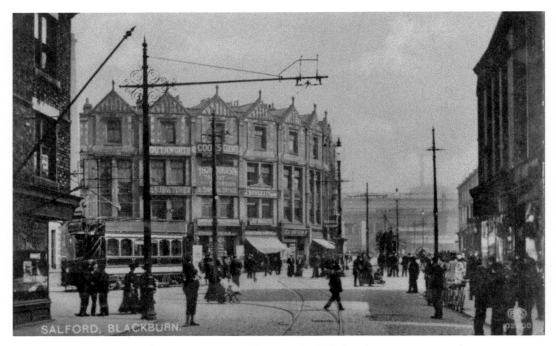

A view further back up Holmes Street in 1916 showing the Wilpshire Tram terminus and numerous shops in the buildings which are still on Salford.

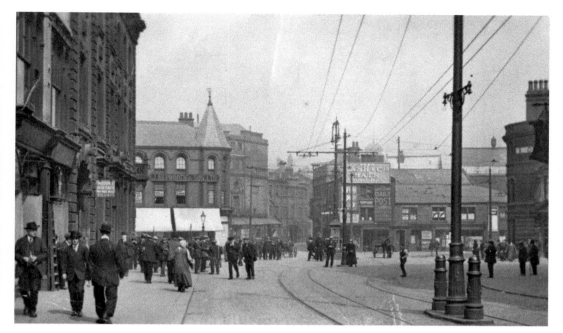

Salford from Railway Road in 1929 – people but no vehicles. Hepworths is facing the camera with the Cinema Royal behind. The Lancashire Evening Post office is under the Cash & Co. advertisement and was here until demolition in the 1960s. The author remembers buying the paper here each day with the 'stop press' (latest news) so recently printed onto the bottom of the back page that the ink was still wet!

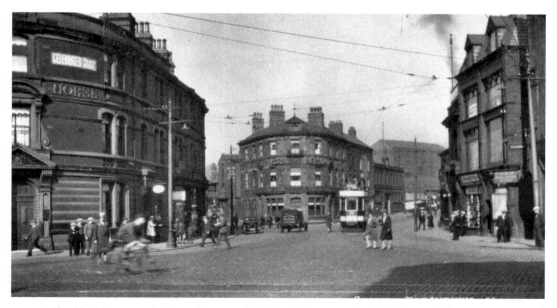

Salford looking towards Penny Street on the left and Eanam to the right, in 1938. The Bay Horse Hotel is on the left and facing is the Lord Nelson Hotel. The Ribble Bus office is in the foreground right with Corrigan's footwear and H. Boyle's house furniture before Ye Olde White Bull Hotel, next to The Weaver to Wearer tailors.

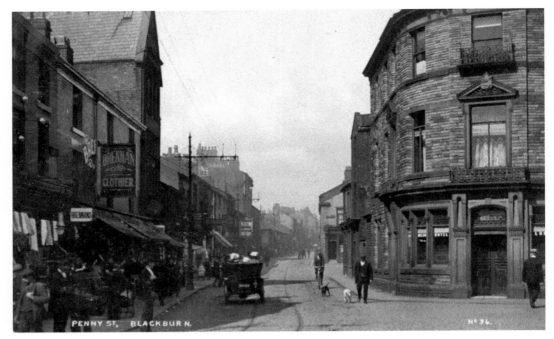

Penny Street from Salford in 1918 with the Lord Nelson Hotel on the right – a much narrower thoroughfare than there is today. The large sign on the middle left indicates Mercer's cheap sofa shop.

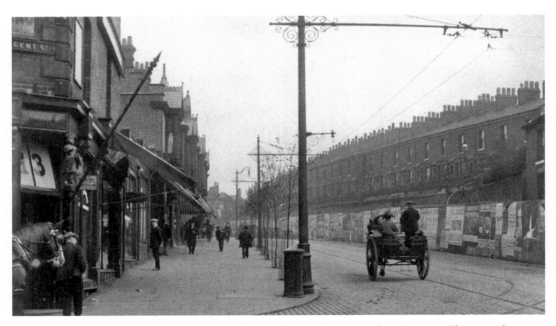

Having gone up Penny Street to Regent Street this was the view that greeted you in 1910. The man who wrote the message on the back of this postcard is also the person standing to the left looking in the shop window – he says so in the message! The nearest shop, on the corner, is that of T. Heaton, tobacconist. The fly posters on the right advertise, among other things, Scarborough, Oxo, circuses, and HP Sauce.

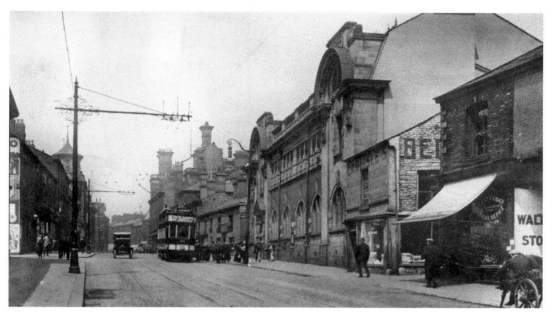

The new post office building (GPO) was built in Darwen Street in 1906. There is a story that the plans for the new Blackpool and Blackburn post offices were accidentally switched! They are quite similar in size and design. The tram is at the Blackburn terminus of the Blackburn-Darwen tramway. Note Eastham's florists on the right with Carlisle's Puritan Lino Company next door. Beyond the post office is the Queen's Head Hotel at the top of Dandy Walk. Opposite is A. Howarth, sewing machine dealers, which closed in 2007.

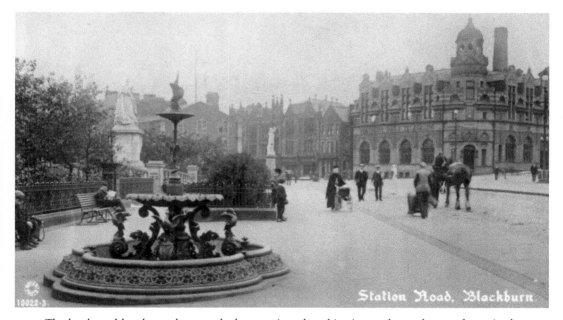

The boulevard has been photographed many times but this picture shows the cast fountain that was there for many years after the unveiling of Queen Victoria's statue in 1911. Ritzema's *Northern Daily Telegraph* building is most impressive.

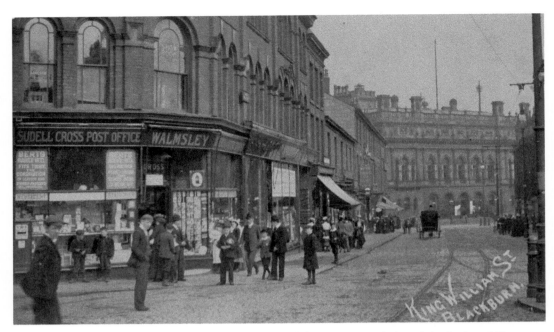

King William Street from Sudell Cross in 1917. A postcard showing postcards for sale in the Post Office window.

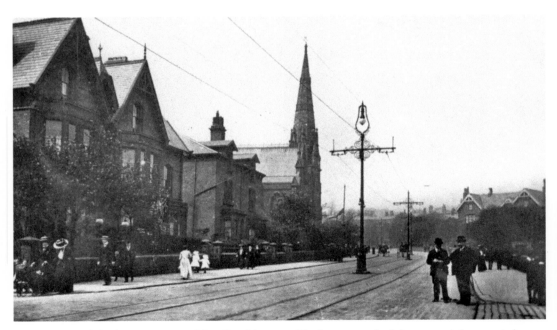

Strawberry Bank looking up Preston New Road in 1910. The houses on the left were mainly occupied by doctors. The elegant St George's Presbyterian church in the distance was built in 1865/6 at a cost of £9,000. It could seat 1,000 people.

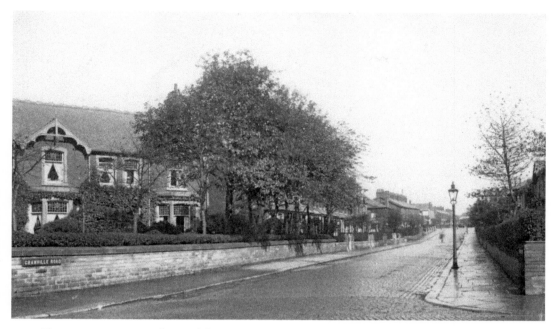

The entrance to Granville Road from Preston New Road in 1929. Very little has changed during the intervening years, apart from the loss of cobbled roadway.

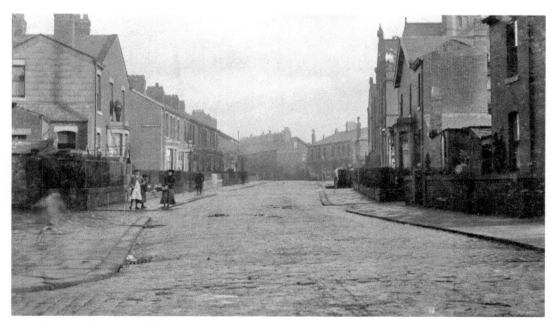

Further along Granville Road in the same year as above at the junction with New Bank Road. Leamington Road Baptist church can be seen to the right.

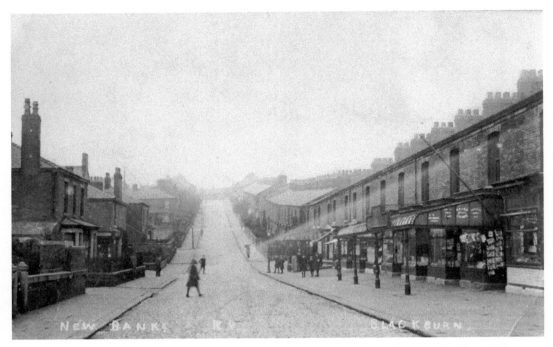

New Bank Road in 1920 when the shops had canopies similar to those in Lord Street at Southport. The shops and the cobbles have changed but little else has.

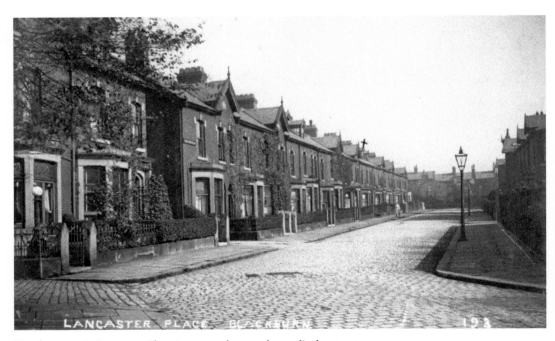

Not far away in Lancaster Place in 1910 when gas lamps lit the street.

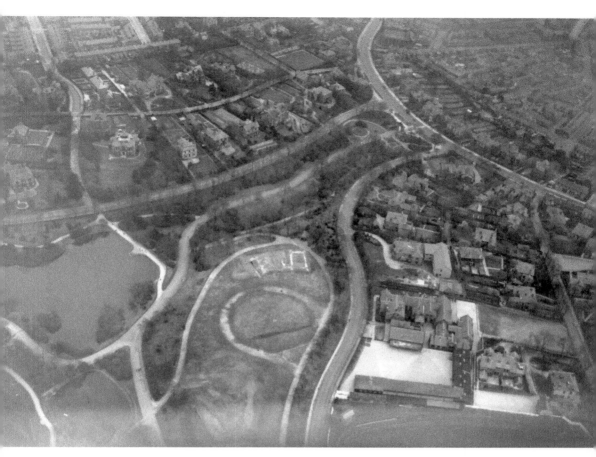

An aerial view from December 1961 in which can be seen the Grammar School, at bottom right, the filled-in band stand in Corporation Park, bottom centre, and the lake to its left. East and West Park roads are prominent with their large houses.

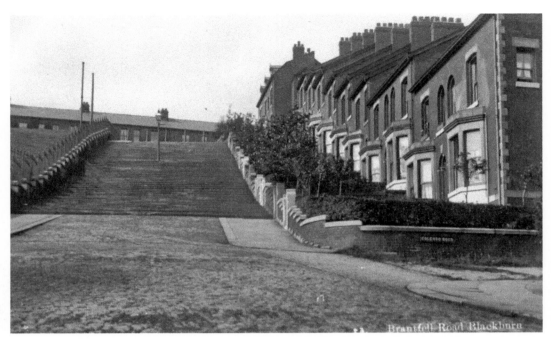

Brantfell Road, better known as 'Sixty Steps'. The park area on the left was still undeveloped.

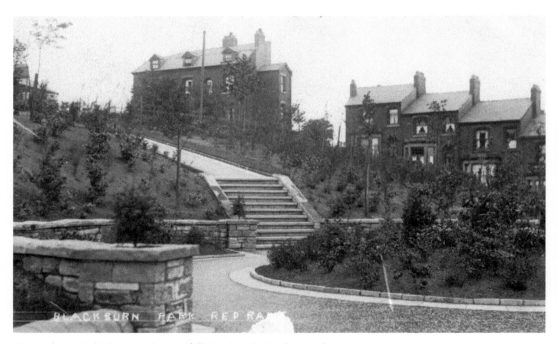

The park newly laid out with Brantfell Road in the background.

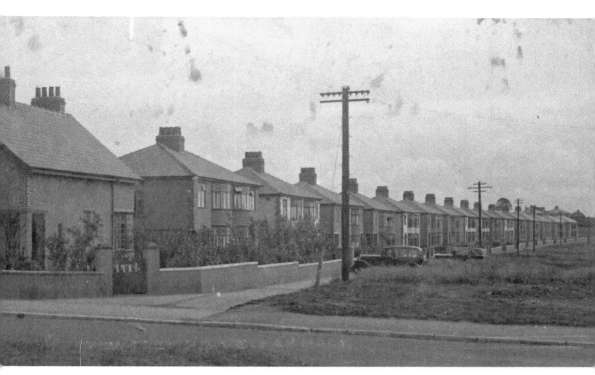

This is a pre-Second World War view of Yew Tree Drive looking from Lammack Road towards Whinney Lane.

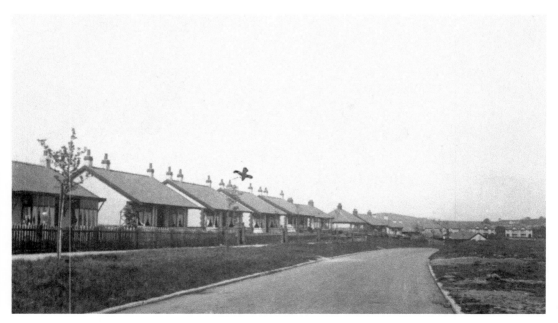

Ramsgreave Drive looking towards Pleckgate Road traffic lights from Lammack.

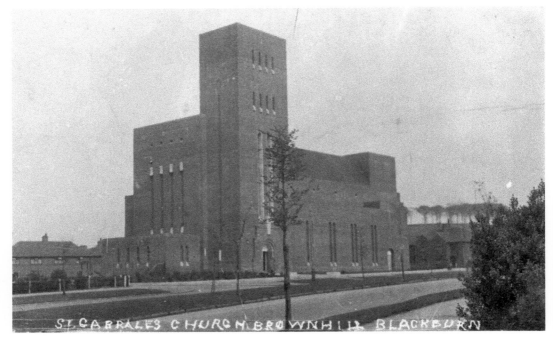

St Gabriels church on Brownhill Drive was designed by F.X. Velarde in the 1930s and hailed as a triumph of modern architecture. In 1969 it came close to being demolished because of hidden defects and it was declared unsafe. The sum of £30,000 was raised to restore it and in 1971 the massive tower was shortened and the flat roofs made into pitched ones. The church survives today.

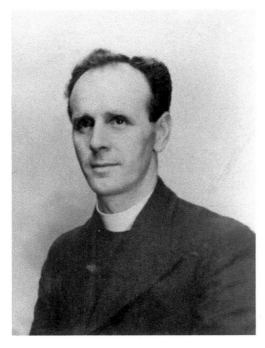

The vicar of St Gabriels, Revd A. Smith, in 1938.

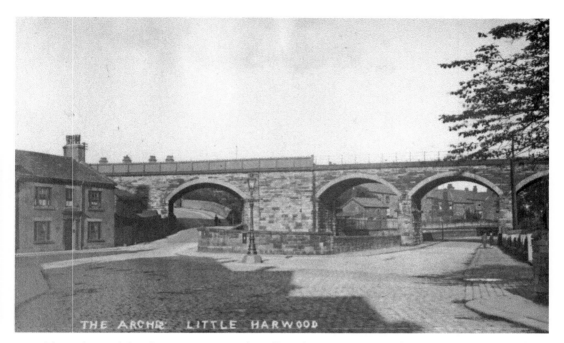

The arches and the Plane Tree Inn at Cob Wall, Little Harwood. Note the lamp post in the middle of the road now replaced by a mini-roundabout. The viaduct has recently been renovated.

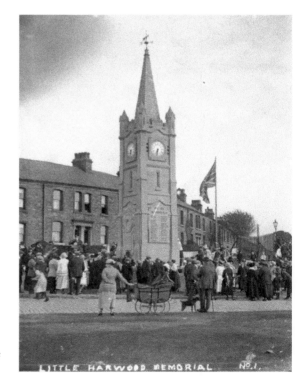

The unveiling of the War Memorial Clock Tower at Little Harwood on 11 August 1923. Major General A. Solly-Flood officiated before 12,000 people. This photograph must have been taken after the crowd dispersed.

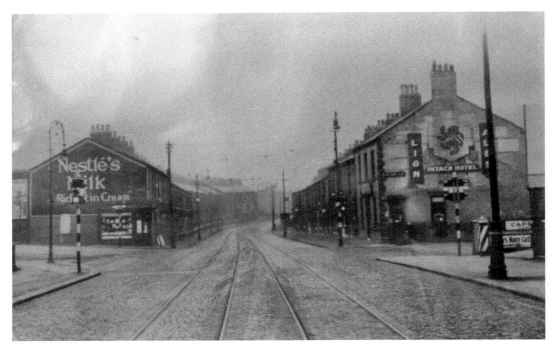

Intack looking towards town with the original traffic lights in place. There is still a barbers here on the right.

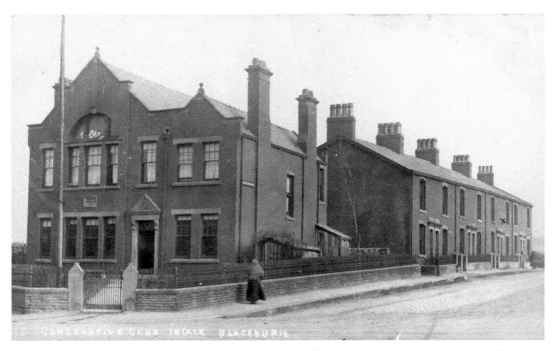

The Intack and Knuzden Conservative Club at the Intack traffic lights in 1907. St Ives is to the right.

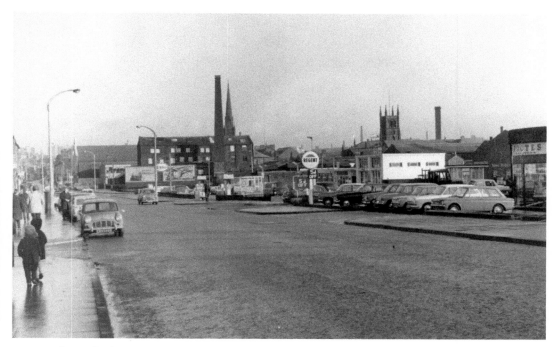

Bank Top looking towards town in the 1960s. The Rootes Group was displaying Hillman and Singer cars on the forecourt. St Peters church, on the right, was later demolished.

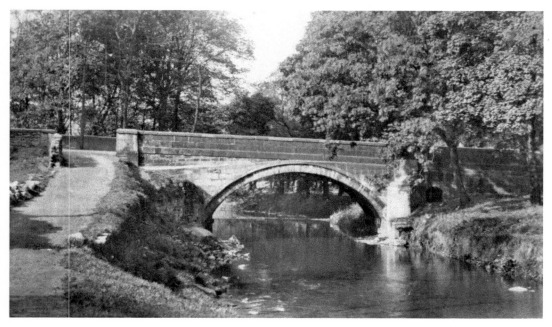

Feniscliffe Bridge near Witton Park in about 1920. The bridge is still there but the site from which the photograph was taken is now occupied by what was the Scapa Group Company building.

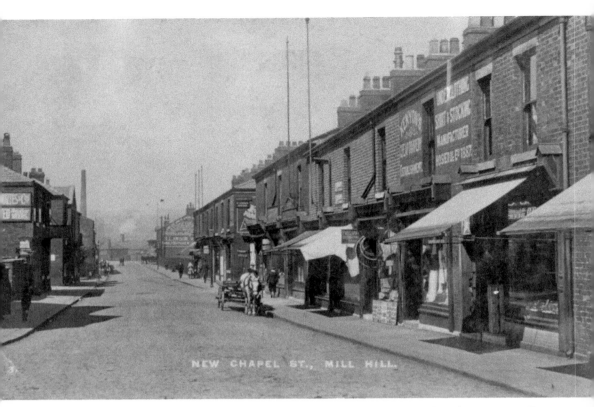

New Chapel Street, Mill Hill, with only a horse and cart for traffic, in 1925. The side street partially hidden behind the horse was Caroline Street and the shops from there were: Miss M.E. Meadows, grocer, George Tennant, Richard Draine, butcher, J. Rawlinson, fruiterer, T. Vipond, confectioner, Robert Wiggins, James Kenyon, draper, and James Heyes, fruiterer. In the distant right can be seen Richard Lawson, butchers. The off-licence of A. Thwaites can be seen on the left. Today this street is still a busy shopping street, only the names have changed.

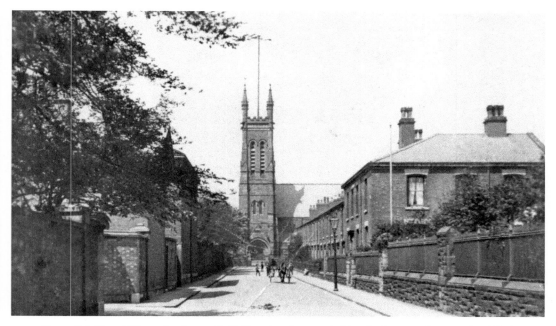

Cavendish Place, Witton, leading to St Philips church, recorded by the Preston photographer Mr Evans.

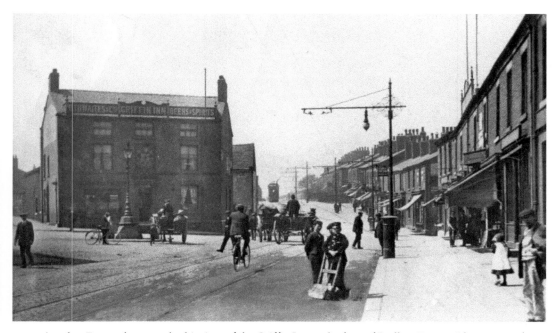

Another Evans photograph, this time of the Griffin Inn at the foot of Redlam Brow with an ornate lamp and horse trough in front. This pub is still a dominating presence on this corner.

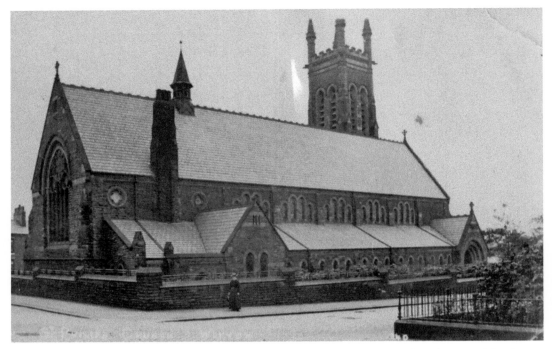

St Philips church at Witton, seen here from Lansdowne Street, was built in 1880 by Adam Dugdale of nearby Griffin Lodge with public subscriptions and the support of local benefactors. The designer was John Lowe of Manchester.

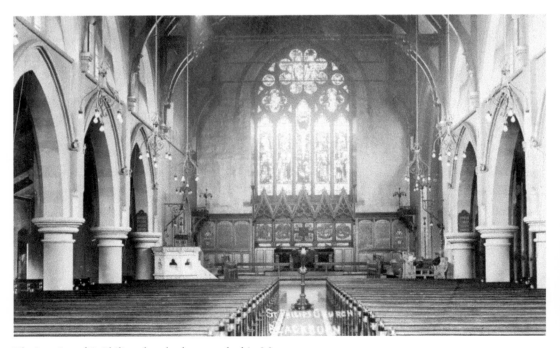

The interior of St Philips church photographed in May 1910.

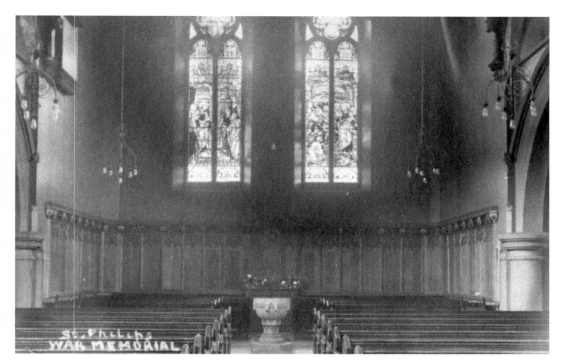

At the back of St Philips church was a wooden screen war memorial recording the names of all those who perished in the two world wars. The church was demolished in the 1970s but the tower was preserved and the stained glass transferred to Christ Church, Burlington, Iowa, USA.

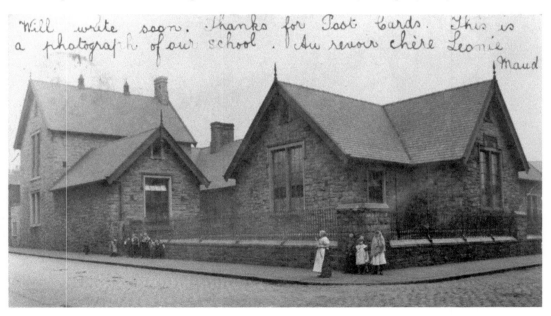

The primary school of St Philips was erected in 1870 and was used as the church until the main one was built. It was more commonly known as the 'Griffin' School but was actually called Dugdales School. This is how it looked in 1905.

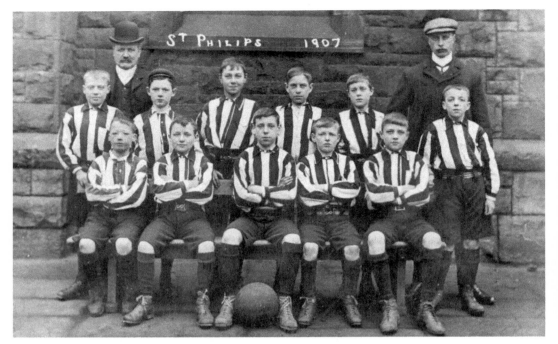

A St Philips School football team of 1907 with the headmaster on the right and the 'coach' on the left.

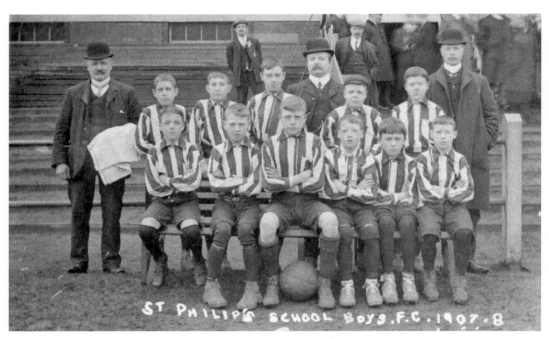

Another school team from St Philips, for the 1907/8 season, believed to have been recorded at Ewood prior to a schoolboys league final match.

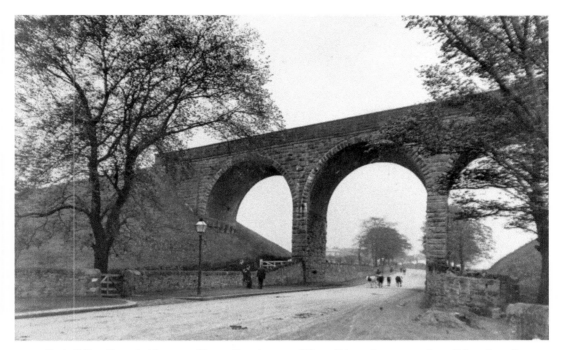

Feniscliffe railway bridge near Cherry Tree in 1904. When did you last see cattle walking along Preston Old Road? The bridge carried a spur line of the railway to the paper mill but it has not been used for many years.

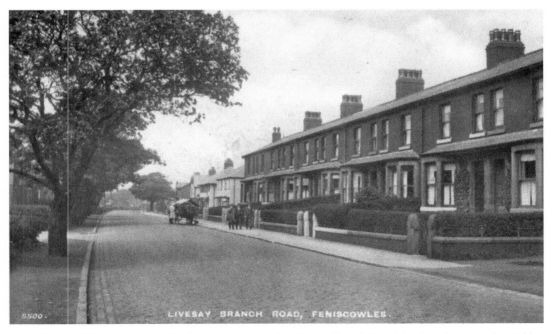

LIVESAY BRANCH ROAD, FENISCOWLES.

Another Evans photograph of the 1920s, showing Livesy Branch Road leading down to the Fielden Arms junction with Preston Old Road. On the right is Park Farm Road.

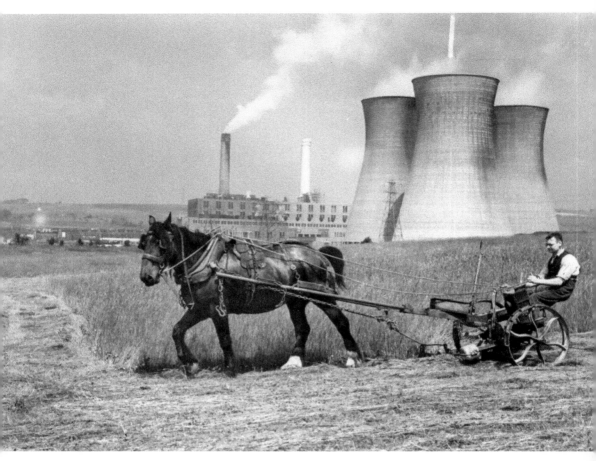

The old meets the new in 1956. Some farms were clearly still using horses when this picture was taken and Whitebirk power station was having a second turbine hall and chimney added.

three

Commerce

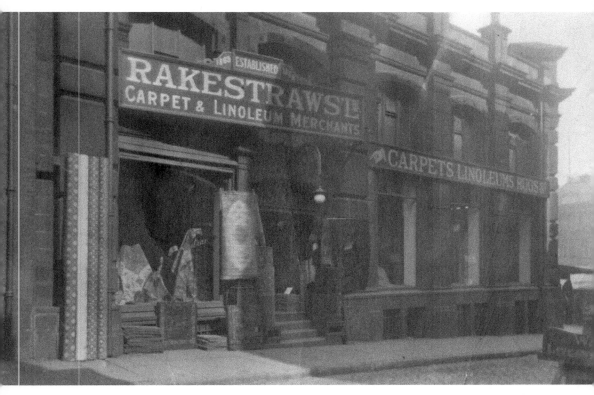

Rakestraw's Emporium of floorcoverings established in 1869 by Christopher Rakestraw on Lord Street, at the top of the old market place.

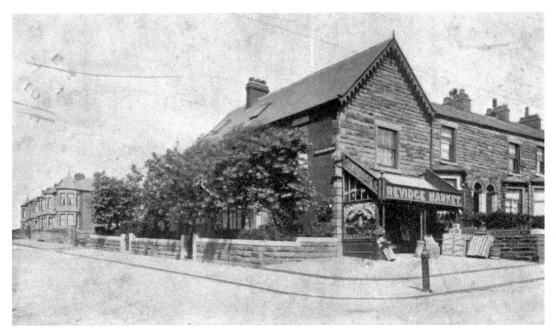

A shop called Revidge Market at the corner of Wycollar Road and Revidge Road in 1907. This postcard photograph was published by Frankland and the shop is now a hairdressers.

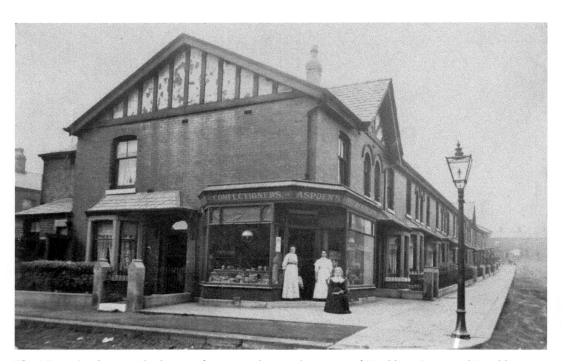

The Misses Aspden outside their confectionery shop at the corner of Markham Street and Franklin Street (Road) Witton in 1915. Note the unmade street surfaces.

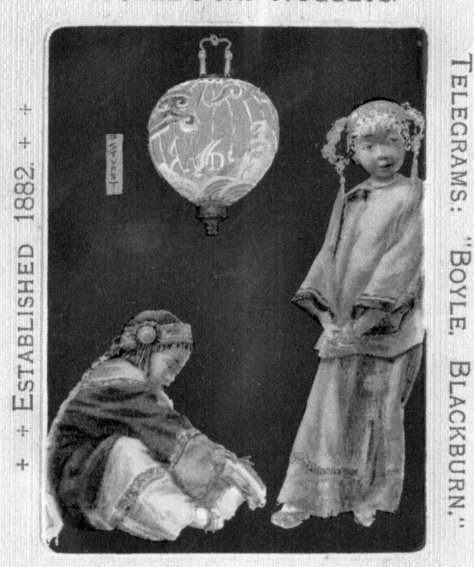

BOYLE'S JAP NUGGETS.

ＥSTABLISHED 1882. + + +

TELEGRAMS: "BOYLE, BLACKBURN."

THE BEST ON EARTH!

Boyle's Jap Nuggets were famous throughout the country. This is one of six beautifully coloured advertising postcards for Messrs Boyle who were established in Blackburn in 1822 (the 1882 date on the card is a misprint). James Boyle was an alderman and confectioner who came originally to Blackburn from Bolton in 1818 and stayed. His story is told in Abram's *Blackburn Characters of a Past Generation*. Although most of his sweet production was in boiled sweets, Jap Nuggets were a type of nougat.

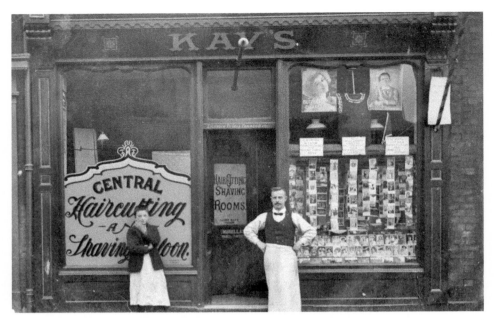

Riley Kay's Central Haircutting and Shaving Saloon, on the left, and, to the right, his postcard shop. The shops were on Victoria Street next to Hilton's shoe shop at the corner of Church Street. By 1974 it had become Whalley's tobacconists.

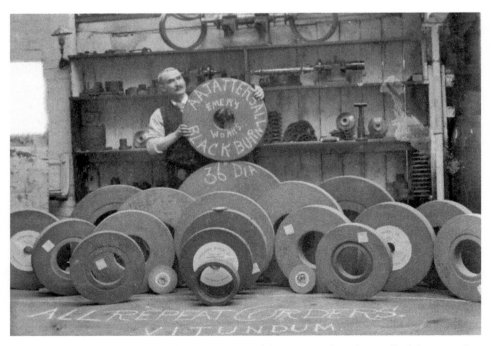

The emery works of A.A. Tattersall display some of their range of products; all of these grinding wheels were apparently 'repeat orders'.

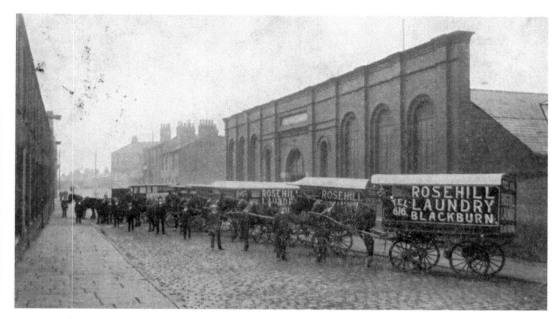

The fleet of Rose Hill Laundry horse-drawn wagons in 1909. The company was on Higher Barns Street, Eanam. It had shops on Eanam and 42 King William Street. They quoted in their advertising, 'We have regular customers sending to us from all over England, Ireland, Scotland, Wales, and Channel Isles, per van, parcels post, and rail ... Give us a Trial.'

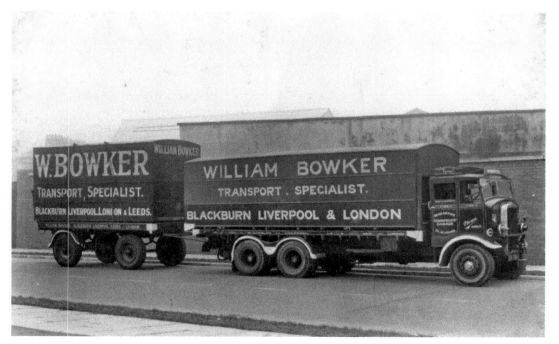

A 1930s long haul William Bowker's lorry and trailer. The modern firm of W.H. Bowker's Haulage began on Stansfeld Street and were classified as 'road, motor transport contractor and general carriers'. Based now at Bamber Bridge, the company is a major, European-wide player.

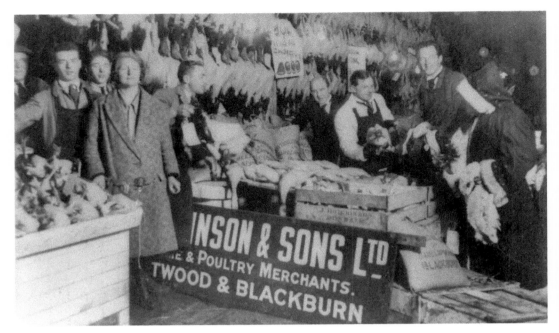

A stall in Blackburn Market of Tomlinson & Sons Ltd of Fleetwood & Blackburn. Ossie Tomlinson can be seen centre back with Vincent second right and Margaret facing fourth left.

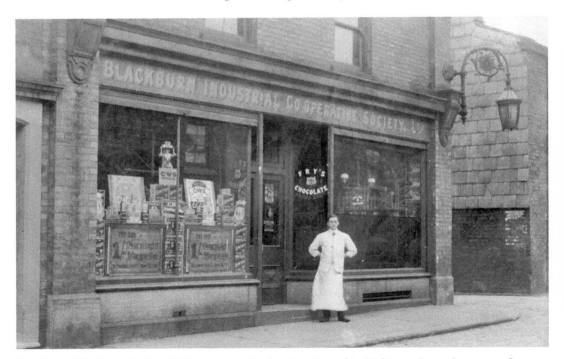

The shop of Blackburn Industrial Co-operative Society Ltd situated in Dickinson Street, June 1910. In 1891 the shop had been the Bank Top Co-operative Store, so it had presumably been merged or taken over. The headquarters of this particular Co-op was on Peter Street.

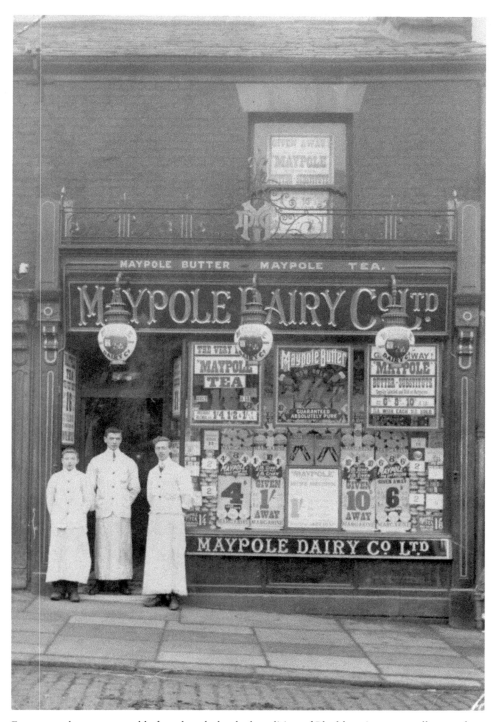

Everyone who was around before the wholesale demolition of Blackburn's centre well remembers the Maypole on Victoria Street. This shop, however, was another branch at No. 2 Bank Top in 1912.

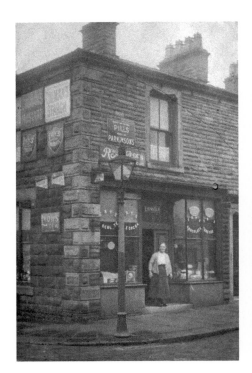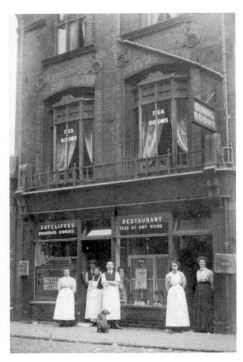

Left: A local shop that had everything. This one was situated on the corner of Inkerman Street and Altom Street. Right: The staff of Sutcliffe's restaurant and tea rooms at 6 Ainsworth Street opposite the Cinema Royal, 1917. The proprietor was Henry Sutcliffe.

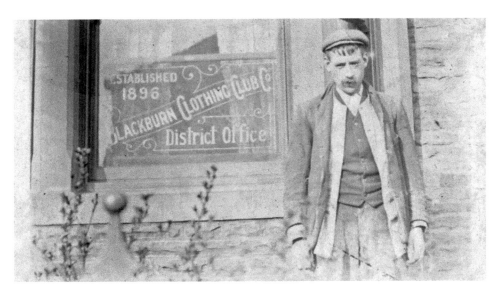

A District Office of the Blackburn Clothing Club Co. whose head office was at Heatley Chambers on Jubilee Street. This office could have been the one at Accrington, Darwen or Clitheroe. The manager at this one does not look a very good advert for the company! The photograph was taken not long after the company was formed in 1896.

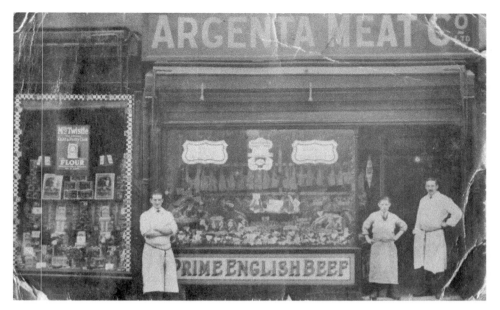

The Argenta Meat Co. had shops in Blackburn on Victoria Street, Higher Eanam and Penny Street in 1915. This is either the Penny Street or Victoria Street one, it being difficult to distinguish from this view because both were situated next to grocer's shops.

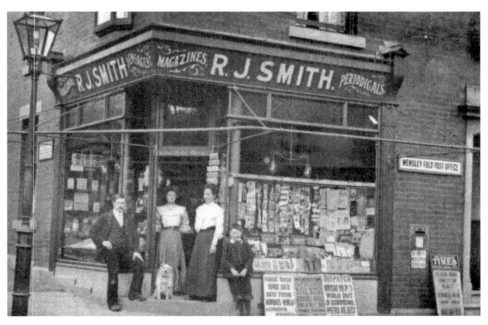

The shop of R.J. Smith and Wensley Fold Post Office on Wensley Street (Road) is still to be seen off Saunders Road at the corner. The posters advertise *Comic Cuts*, *Home Chat*, *Boys' Friend*, *Woman's World*, *Horner's Stories*, *Dispatch*, *The Sporting Chronicle*, and *The Blackburn Times* and there are lots of postcards on display in the window.

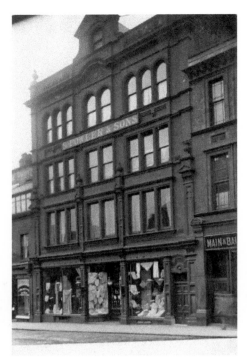

S. Fowler & Sons, dress, costume and mantle makers, furriers and funeral undertakers, 1910. The building still stands today in Preston New Road but without the top floor and parapet seen here. By 1915 it was Thompson Bros, electrical engineers and was known as the Royal Buildings. To the left is J. Holroyd & Co. Ltd, dyers, and the famous Burton & Yarland photographic studios are above.

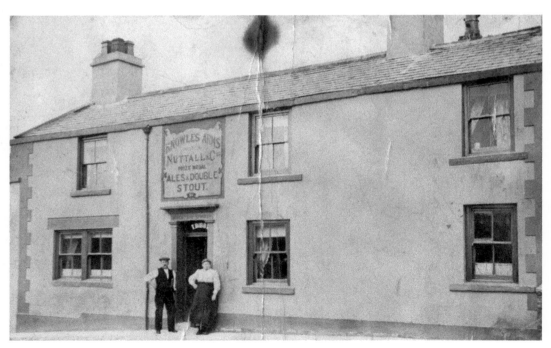

The old Knowles Arms (the Folly) on Pleckgate Road long before demolition and replacement. The landlord, Thomas Bibby, and his wife are seen here posing under their licence board. He was still licensee in 1915, some years after this photograph was taken.

four

People

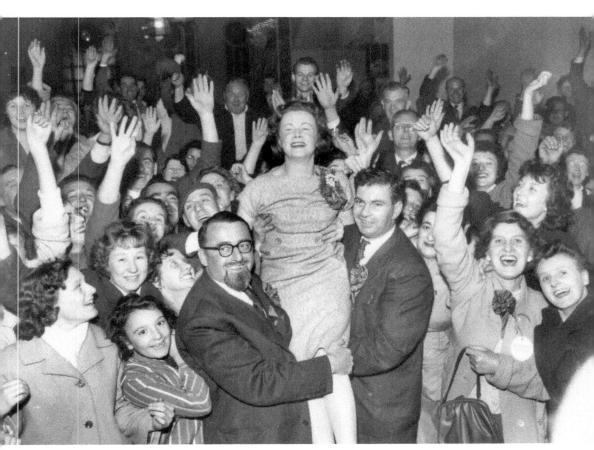

Barbara Castle (now Baroness), Labour MP for Blackburn, on her election night in October 1959 with her agent Roy Martin and supporters. She was Blackburn's MP for thirty-four years and then became a member of the European Parliament.

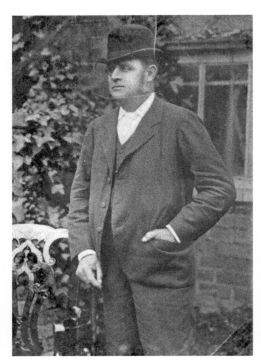

Alderman Sir William Henry (Harry) Hornby
Jnr Bart. JP, MP was Conservative Member of
Parliament for Blackburn from 1886 to 1910
and Mayor of Blackburn in 1876/7 and again
in 1901/2. He helped found the East Lancashire
Cricket Club and was president at Pleasington
golf club as well as being a member of many other
organisations. He was well known as 'Sir Harry'
and also 'Th'owd Gam' Cock'.

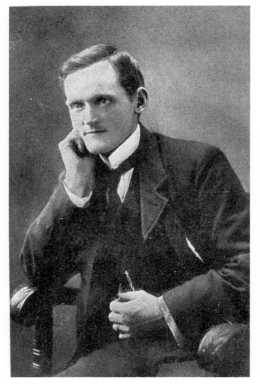

1st Viscount Phillip Snowden, born at Cowling,
West Yorkshire, was Labour Member of
Parliament for Blackburn from 1906 to 1918.
He became Chancellor of the Exchequer in 1924
and again from 1929 to 1931, he was Lord Privy
Seal in the Nationalist Government of 1931 and
resigned in 1932.

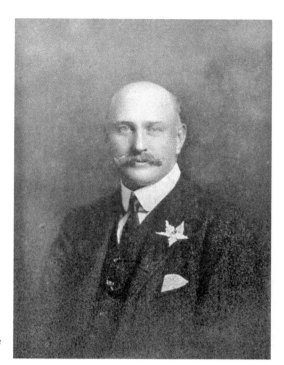

Col. Sir John Rutherford, Bart. JP, MP, DL.
Born in John Street, Blackburn, of Scottish
parentage he was MP for Darwen from 1895
to 1922 and Mayor of Blackburn in 1888/9.
He played football for the Rovers, was a
sprinter and a member of Pleasington and
Wilpshire Golf Clubs. He raced horses and his
horse Solario won the St Leger in 1925 and the
Ascot Gold Cup and Coronation Cup in 1926.

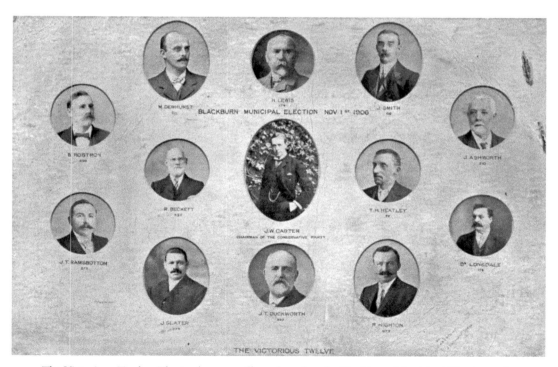

The Victorious Twelve. The twelve councillors elected at the Blackburn Municipal Elections of
1 November 1906.

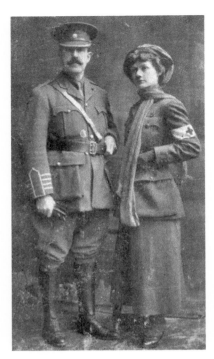

Major Sir Henry Norman, Bart. and Lady Norman pictured here in uniform during the 1914-18 war. He was MP for Blackburn from 1910 to 1923. Although living in London he became a member of the Union Club and was MP for thirteen years.

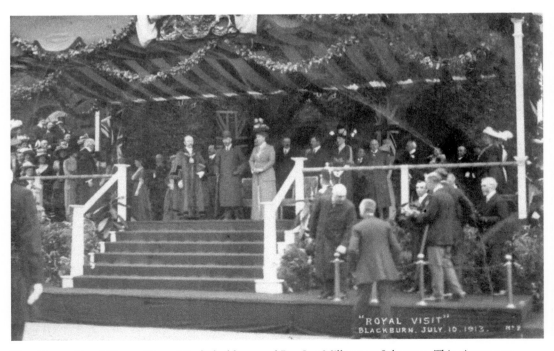

"ROYAL VISIT"
BLACKBURN. JULY 10. 1913.

King George V and Queen Mary visited Blackburn and Roe Lee Mills on 10 July 1913. This picture was taken outside the town hall and shows the royal couple with the mayor John Higginson. The ceremony was the laying of the foundation stone of the public halls.

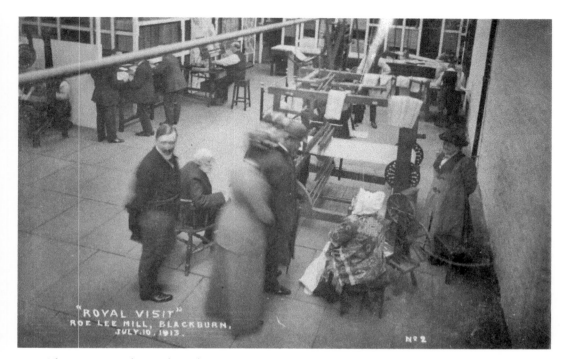

The co-owner John Duckworth is seen presenting the royal pair to the last of the hand loom weavers who had been brought into the mill to demonstrate their now redundant skills on the occasion of the visit. The hand loom weavers lived in the cottages at Green Gown off Pleckgate Road.

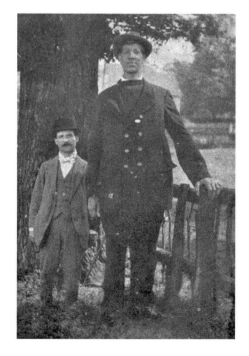

John Fred Kempster was born in Bayswater, London and came to Blackburn as a fairground attraction. He was a famous giant, his height being listed at different times as between 7 ft 8½ in and 8 ft 4 ½ in. This photograph from a postcard shows him at the age of nineteen years. The height of 7 ft 4 in has been pencilled onto the corner of this card. He lit cigarettes from street lamps and could pass old pennies through his signet ring. He was twenty nine years old when he lodged at the Haymarket Hotel for the annual Easter Fair. He caught pneumonia and died in Queen's Park Hospital on 15 April 1918 and is buried in Blackburn cemetery.

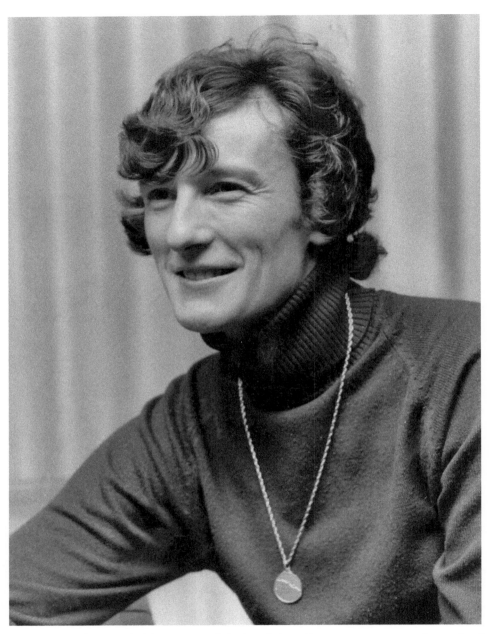

Bolton-born Julie Greenhalgh was one of the best lady golfers ever to represent the north of England but perhaps did not earn the recognition she deserved. She was an honorary member of Pleasington, Killarney, and Ganton golf clubs and her achievements were exceptional: Home International Player in 1960-61, 1963, 1966-67, 1970-71, 1975-78; European Ladies Team Championships 1971-77; Curtis Cup Player 1964, 1970, 1974, 1976, 1978; Vagliano Trophy 1961, 1965, 1975, 1977; Espirito Santo Captain 1970-74; Commonwealth Tournament 1963; British Strokeplay Championship 1974-75; English Ladies' 1961-62; DAKS Woman Golfer of the Year 1974, all in addition to her Lancashire Ladies' feats and Junior Golf successes. She is now Julie Merrill and lives in Lancaster.

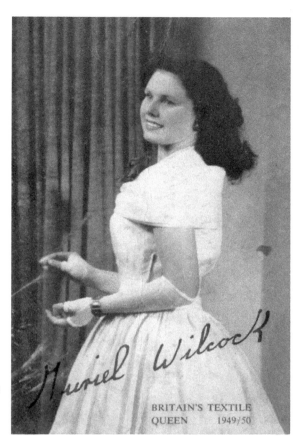

Muriel Wilcock was selected to be Britain's Textile Queen in 1949. This is a postcard sponsored by The Blackburn Pioneer Mill Ltd of Mill Hill, Blackburn.

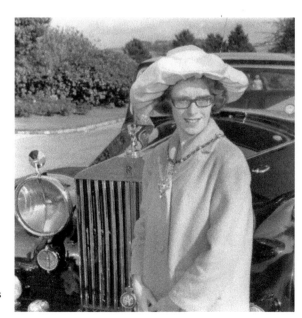

Madge Hindle better known as 'Renie', wife of Alf Roberts the owner of the corner shop in *Coronation Street*. Madge, born in Blackburn, is married to retired Blackburn solicitor Michael Hindle and they live in Settle. She is pictured here as Mayoress of Blackburn in 1966 when Mrs E. Railton was mayor of the borough.

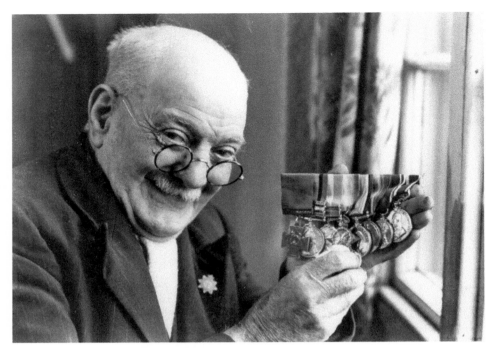

James Pitts VC photographed in 1956. He was Blackburn's first and, at the time of the photograph, also the oldest VC winner. He lived in Duckworth Street. He won his VC during the Boer War at Ladysmith on 6 January 1900 when as a private in the 1st Battalion Manchester Regiment he and a companion, Pte Robert Scott of Haslingden, took part in a stand which held the Boers long enough to allow Lord Roberts to enter the Free State and bring relief to Ladysmith. His companion also won the VC. He died in 1980 at the age of 77.

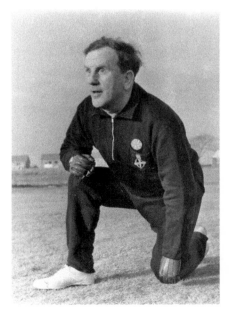

Bill Griffiths photographed in 1969. Bill was captured by the Japanese in Java in 1942 and suffered horrific injuries after being ordered to uncover a booby trapped ammunition dump. He lost his sight, both hands, and severely damaged a leg. He was selected as Disabled Sportsman of the Year in 1969 and was awarded an MBE in 1977. In 1995 Blackburn Borough awarded him their Civic Medal at a ceremony marking fifty years of peace.

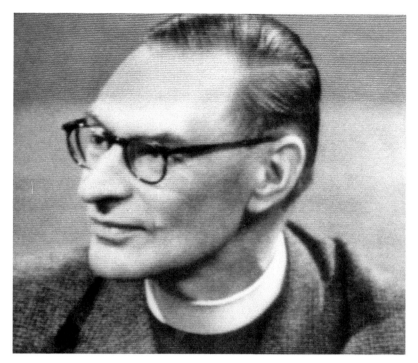

The Revd Dr Chad Varah during a television appearance in 1961. He was at Holy Trinity church in the 1940s and founded the Samaritans in 1970 after working in London with the despairing and suicidal.

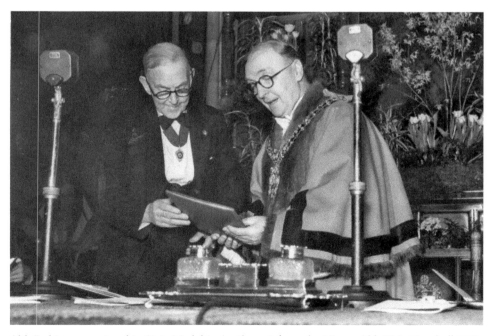

Ald. Robinson receives his Civic Medal in April 1956 from the Mayor Ald. W.A. Henshall MC.

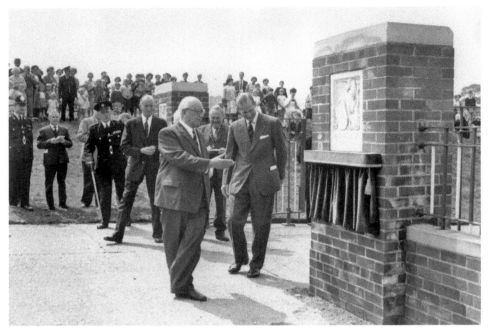

The Duke of Edinburgh arrives at the entrance to King George's Fields, Pleasington, to officially open them on 5 July 1963. He is accompanied by Alderman J. Stirrup JP.

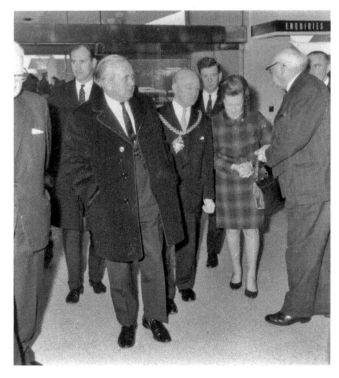

Prime Minister Harold Wilson arrives to open Blackburn Technical College in January 1970 accompanied by Barbara Castle, MP for Blackburn, the Mayor E. Gregson and Ald. Eddie JP.

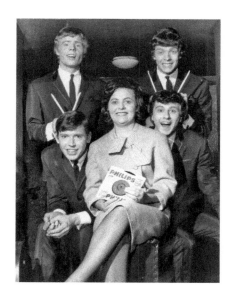

The Blackburn pop group, The Four Pennies, with leader Lionel Morton (back right), pose with Mrs Reidy following the success of their hit record *Juliet*. Lionel was a cathedral chorister before becoming a professional singer. Mrs Reidy was the proprietor of Reidy's Music in Penny Street, later Darwen Street.

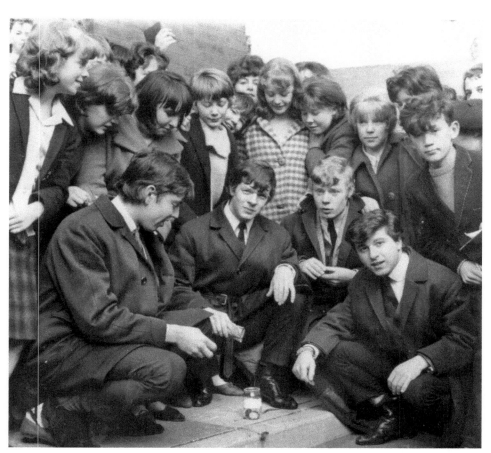

The Four Pennies with pupils at St James' church in 1964.

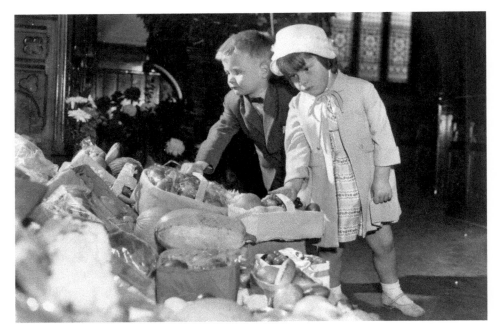

Children of Audley Range Congregational church place their gifts at the harvest festival in September 1963.

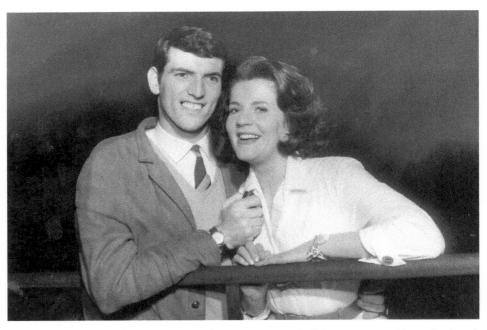

Derek Dougan and Valerie Martin on their engagement in February 1960. Alexander Derek Dougan had been signed from Portsmouth by Blackburn Rovers as a centre forward in March 1959. Valerie was a well-known local beauty queen. Derek handed in a transfer request on the way to Wembley in 1960 and in August 1961 he was sold to Aston Villa.

five

Church and Education

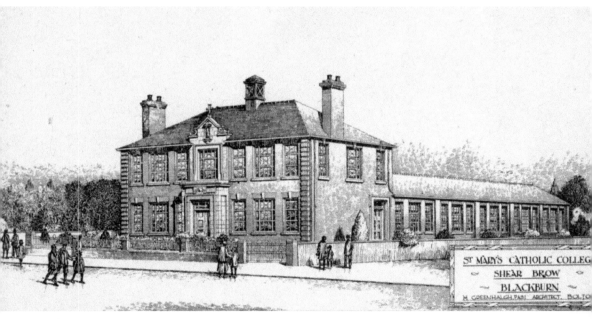

An architect's sketch of St Mary's Catholic College, Shear Brow, made by H. Greenhalgh of Bolton. The college was opened in November 1930 by Bishop Henshaw and cost £8,000. The building plot of five acres had been bought for £2,650 and the college accommodated 150 students. It was recognised by the Board of Education at the end of the following year. The school had been started by Marist Fathers in 1925 at Springfield, Shear Bank Road, at the invitation of Bishop Casartelli with the object of providing a Catholic secondary school for Blackburn and the neighbourhood. In the 1950s it was designated a secondary grammar school for Blackburn and in more recent times it has become a sixth form college.

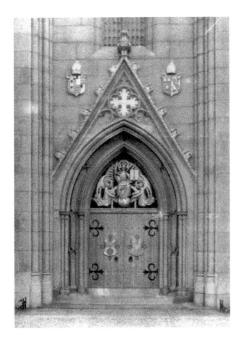

The refurbished cathedral door in 1963. When a new bishop is installed at a cathedral he has to knock on the door three times with his staff to gain admittance.

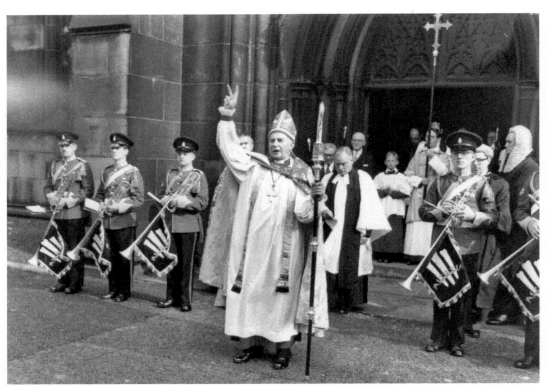

The 4th Bishop of Blackburn Dr Charles Robert Claxton after his installation service in October 1960, presenting himself to the crowds outside the cathedral.

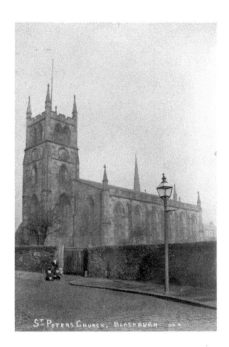

St Peter's church, St Peter's Street, was erected in 1820/21 at a cost of £13,000. It faced the old grammar school on Freckleton Street but all that remains of it today is the churchyard. This Shaw photograph is of 1910.

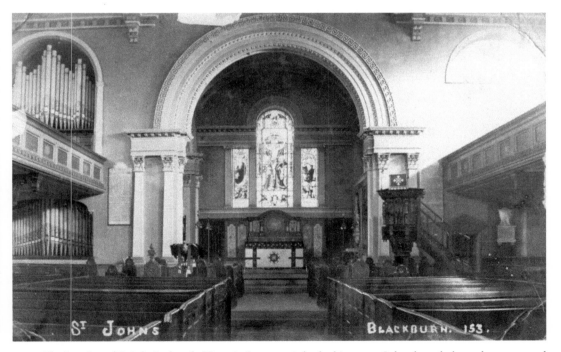

The interior of St John's church, Victoria Street, as it looked in 1914. It has latterly been deconsecrated and became the offices of the Citizen's Advice Bureau. It was erected in 1788/9 at a cost of £8,000. The organ chamber on the left was built in 1890 with an organ on the tubular pneumatic principle at a cost of £570.

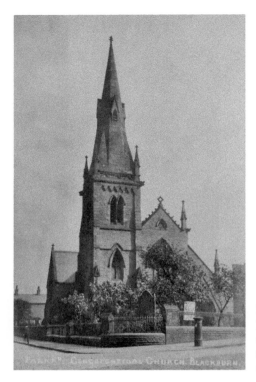

Park Road Congregational church, built in the Late Decorated style, is seen here in 1905. Now demolished, it stood at the corner of Houghton Street and Park Place, Grimshaw Park. It was erected in 1858 at a cost of £5,000.

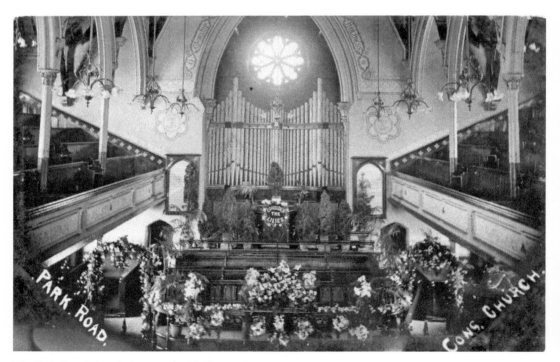

The Park Road church decorated with flowers in 1905.

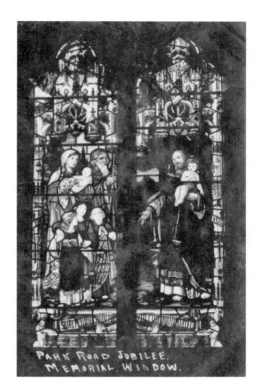

Two of the beautiful stained glass windows at Park Road commemorating the Park Road Jubilee in 1908. The first depicts Jesus saying, 'Suffer little children to come unto me' and the second, 'Ye that sheweth mercy on him'.

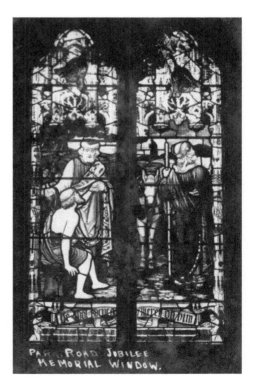

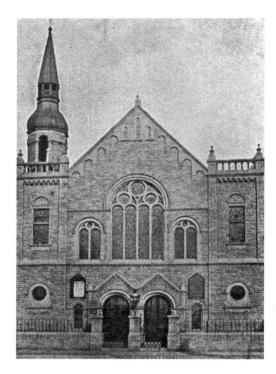

The Primitive Methodist church on Montague Street in 1912. Dating from 1837 it was rebuilt in 1891 at a cost of £2,300 from a design by R. Dixon of Oldham.

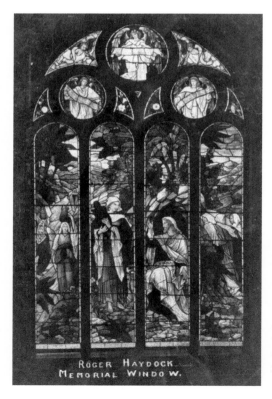

ROGER HAYDOCK
MEMORIAL WINDOW.

Roger Haydock, 'Owd Roger', was a well known Primitive Methodist lay preacher and Bible colporteur. For sixty-three years he was a member of the Montague Street Primitive Methodist church. He was born on 26 December 1809 in Clayton-le-Dale. He became a weaver in Blackburn, and the memorial window was unveiled twelve months after his death at the age of 94. The church was demolished along with many other buildings in Montague Street in the 1960s.

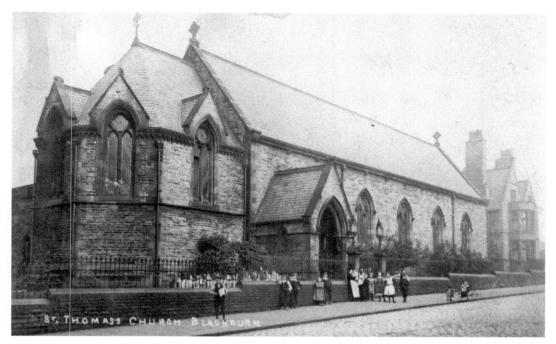

A pre-First World War photograph of St Thomas' church on Lambeth Street. It was designed by Mr E.G. Paley of Lancaster and was erected in 1865 at a cost of £5,600 and could seat 1,054 people. It is now demolished but the school was reprieved.

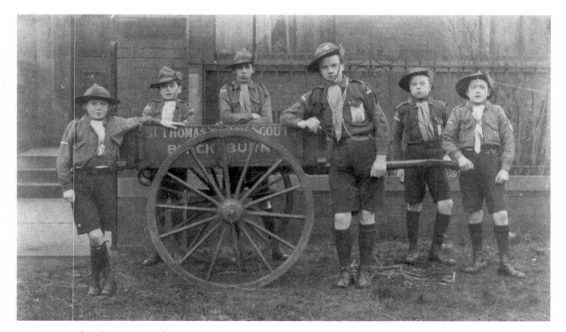

An early photograph of St Thomas' scouts with their trek-cart ready to walk to their summer camp, possibly at Hacking Boat.

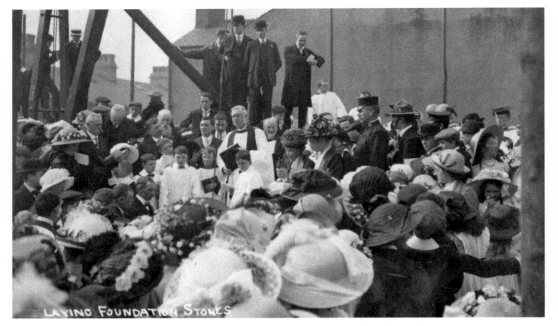

The caption written on this postcard picture states that this event is the laying of the foundation stones for St Andrew's new church but it is probably for the junior school because the new church had already been built in 1877.

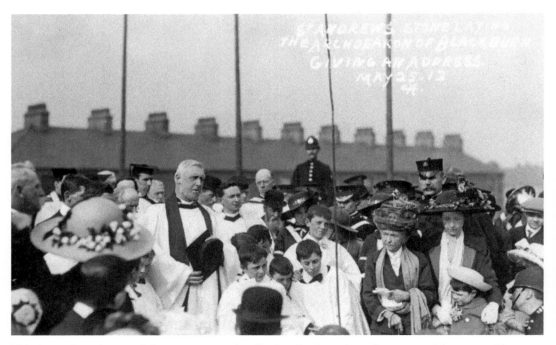

This is another picture of the same event, described as having taken place on 12 May 1912. The Archdeacon of Blackburn is giving an address.

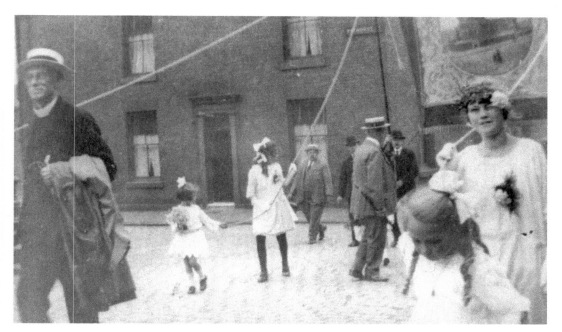

It was common in Whit Week to walk the boundaries of the parish and this photograph from about 1910 shows a procession of the congregation St Paul's 'beating the bounds', at the junction of New Park Street and Bathurst Street.

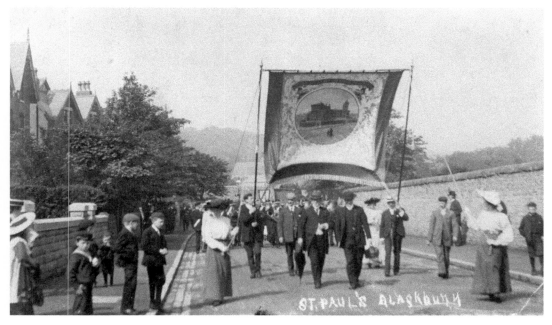

This is another St Paul's Whit walk of around the same period as the one above but not the same year. The walkers are approaching Duke's Brow from West Park Road with the Alexandra Meadows' wall on the right. The banner depicts the St Paul's church building.

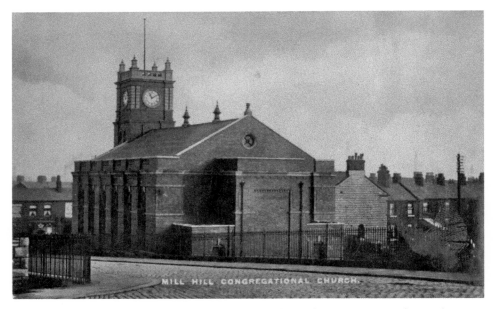

Mill Hill Congregational church was built in 1859 and seated a congregation of 950. The tower was added in 1912 with a clock and Cambridge Chimes completing the development in 1931. It was demolished to build the offices of the Netlon Company.

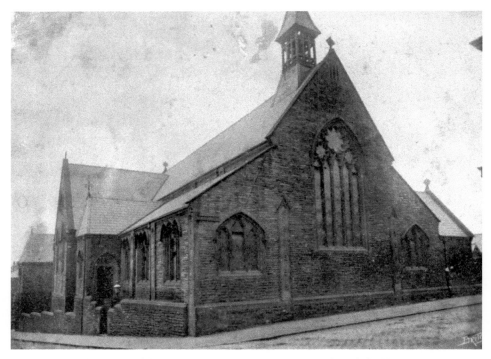

St Barnabas's church on Addison Street. Designed by Mr W.S. Varley of Blackburn, it was erected in 1885-6 at a cost of £6,500 and accommodated 722 worshippers.

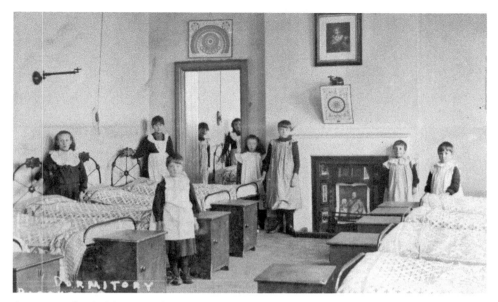

A view inside Blackburn Orphanage at Wilpshire over ninety years ago. The foundation stone was laid on 31 August 1889 and it was opened on 23 July 1891. James Dixon, who started the orphanage, wrote about his experiences in a book, *The Story of the Blackburn Samaritan*. Today it is run by the Blackburn Children's Homes on different lines and is known as the Homestead.

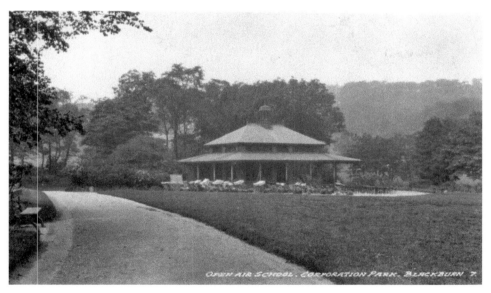

This was the Open Air School situated in Corporation Park near the old bandstand on West Park Road and seen here in 1938. Chest complaints were very common and this is where children were sent to recover, with lots of fresh air. The building is in use today for a playgroup. Many years ago the Open Air School was moved to Roman Road and formed part of three special schools on that site.

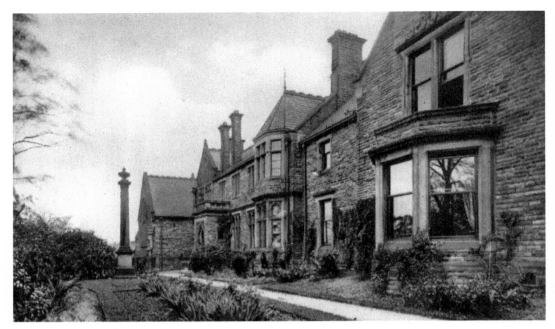

Queen Elizabeth's Grammar School on West Park Road was given its charter in 1567. It moved to its present site in 1884 and has grown to become a nationally acknowledged independent school. This pre-Second World War photograph shows the south east frontage housing the library.

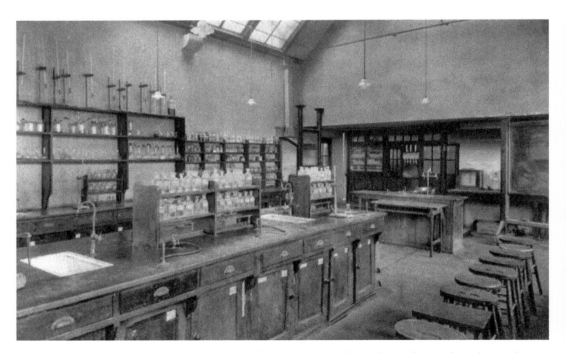

This is the chemistry laboratory in the 1940s. It has been completely modernised since these days and the early 1950s, when the author was a pupil here.

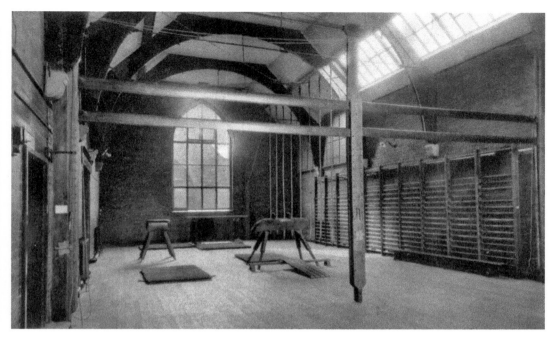

No one who attended Queen Elizabeth's Grammar School in those earlier days will forget the gymnasium and the punishment schools held there by the prefects.

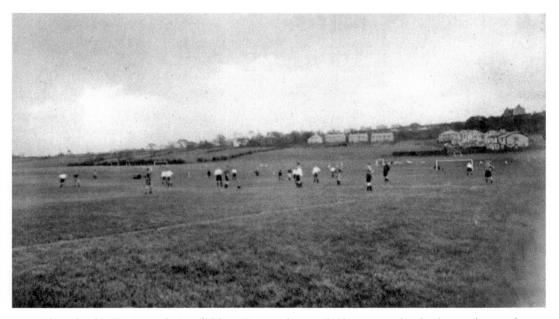

The school's Harrison playing fields at Lammack were built as a result of a legacy from a former mayor of Blackburn, Henry Harrison JP, who, along with his wife, was also responsible for the Harrison Gymnasium and Institute for Girls in Hollins Street. Another public bequest included the East Lancashire Royal Infirmary Nurses' Home.

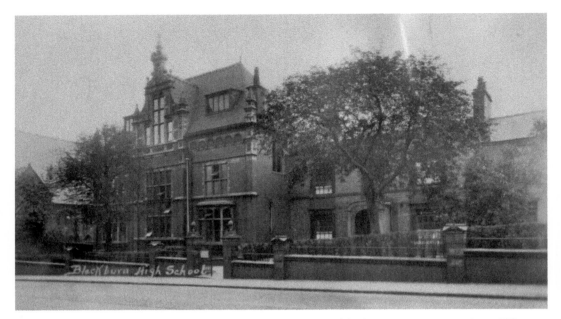

The site of Blackburn High School for Girls in 1907. The school had spent two years at Cross Hill before moving to Preston New Road in the 1940s. The house 'Spring Mount' formed the central part of the school and was built by Councillor James B.S. Sturdy JP, a mayor of Blackburn in 1862/3. The school merged with Witton Park Secondary on Buncer Lane in 1968 but the buildings are still used by the borough and county for educational training purposes.

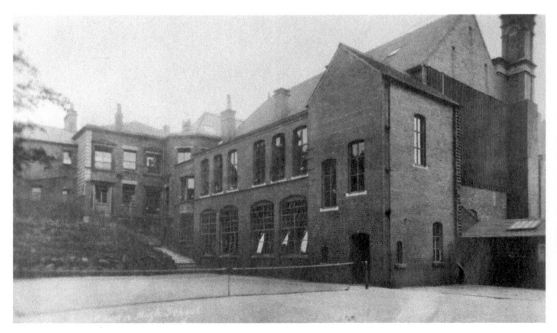

The bottom playground at the High School showing the back of the house and the building containing the big hall and gymnasium.

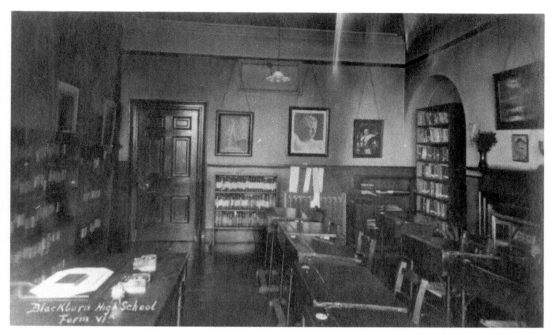

A classroom for Form VI with the old desks that many will remember. Note how small the classroom is.

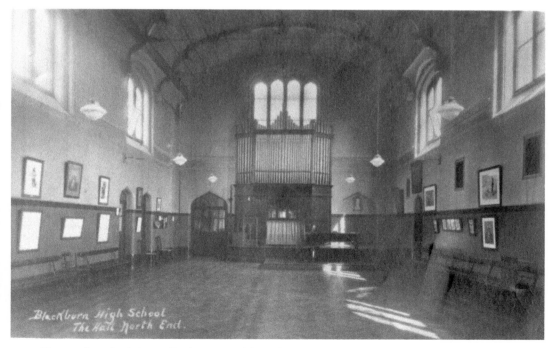

The north end of the Hall where assembly took place. Dances were held here and pupils from the grammar school were invited as well.

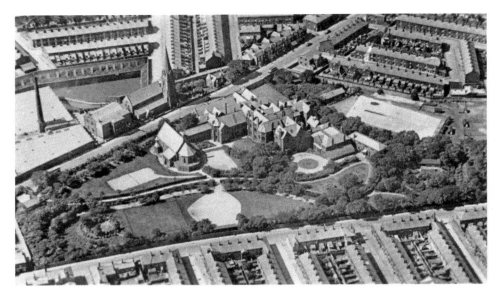

An aerial view of the Notre Dame Grammar School, commonly known as the Convent, on Whalley New Road. It was demolished in 1990 and the site is now occupied by a new housing estate. It was set up by the sisters of Notre Dame de Namur who arrived at St Alban's church from France in 1850. The Brookhouse buildings were commenced in 1859 and the school was merged with John Rigby High School and closed in 1987.

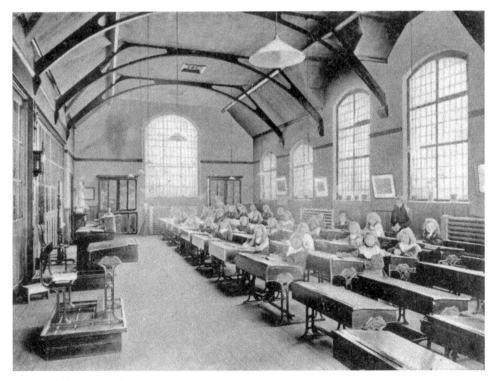

A typical classroom of 1904.

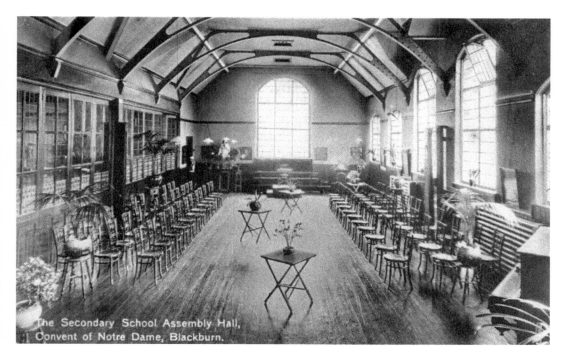

The Assembly Hall for the secondary school pupils in 1904.

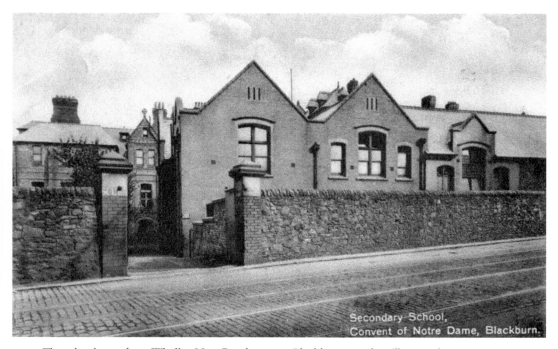

The school seen from Whalley New Road as most Blackburn people will remember it.

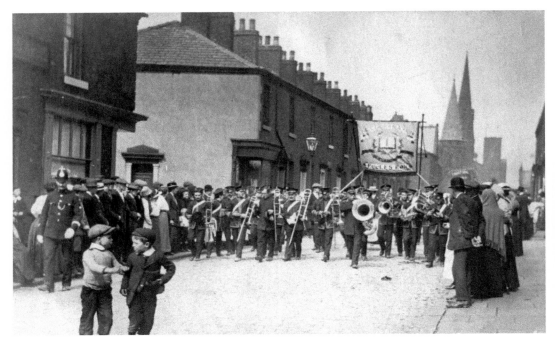

Eccles Row Mission Sunday School of Shorrock Street, Grimshaw Park, walk with their banner and band in procession with other churches along Mosley Street to a Field Day, *c.* 1910.

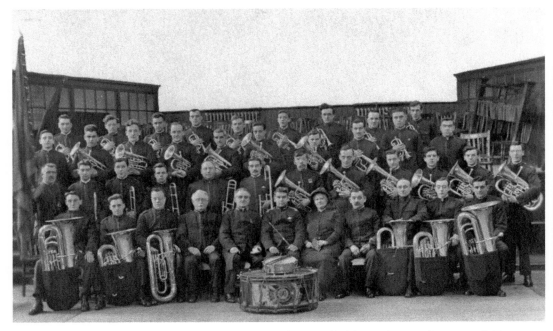

The band of Blackburn Citadel, the Salvation Army, photographed by Leslie's Studios at Bank Top, *c.* 1910. The bandmaster is a Mr Anderton and Major and Mrs Munns were in charge.

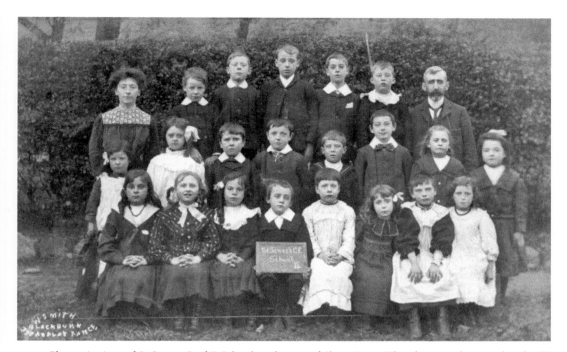

Class 4 juniors of St James C of E School at the top of Shear Brow. The photograph was taken by W. Smith of Audley Range sometime before 1918. The St James National and Sunday Schools were built in 1877 and enlarged in 1895.

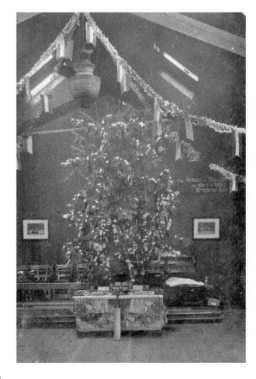

The Church Army Hall decorated for Christmas 1909. Their main public hall was in Merchant Street off Ainsworth Street and accommodated 1,000 people with a hall in Cowell Street and also Ordnance Street and Moorgate Street, Livesey. The Christmas tree has gifts laid out below it for distribution to the poor children of the borough.

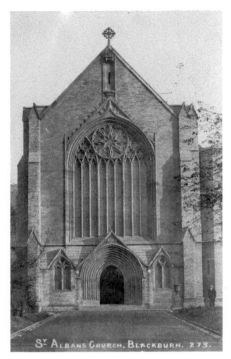

An A. J. W. Shaw photograph of St Alban's RC church as it looked in about 1910. Its history goes back to 1773 but this edifice (the fourth), a Decorated Gothic style building, wasn't opened until 1901 by the Bishop of Salford. It was designed by Edward Goldie of London and was built by John Boland of Blackburn at a cost of £20,000, excluding the tower and spire. It seated 1,000 people.

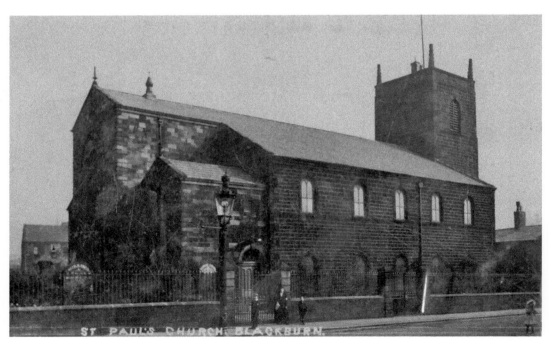

Another A. J.W. Shaw photograph of about 1910 showing St Paul's church on Nab Lane of which only the graveyard remains as a garden for the Blackburn College. It was first opened as a chapel of ease in 1791 and was consecrated in 1829. It was built in a very plain style.

six

Leisure, Entertainment and Sport

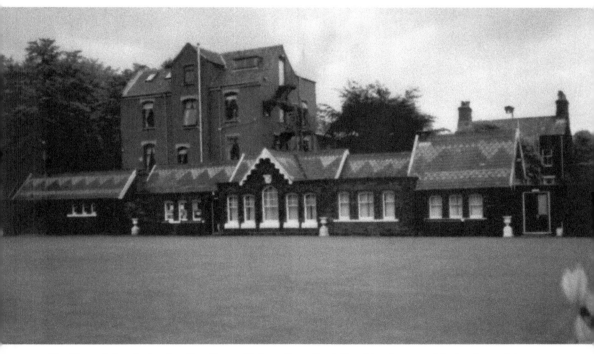

Blackburn Subscription Bowling Green Club on Shear Bank Road has been on this site since 1867 but before that, and since 1847, was in St Peter Street, behind the old Grammar School. Even earlier it was at Cicely Hole until construction of the new railway station. The club's records date back to 1749 but on good authority the club was in being before that. The name of the first steward recorded is John Sudell of Woodfold Park in 1754. For many years it was also the home of Blackburn Curling Club which won many honours and whose trophies can still be seen on display.

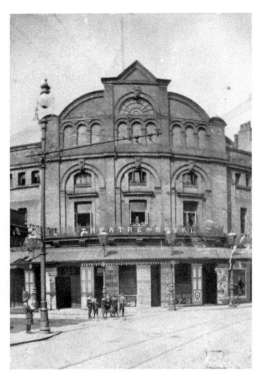

The Theatre Royal and Opera House on Ainsworth Street in 1908. It later became the Cinema Royal. The original theatre was built in 1816 and it was then rebuilt in 1867. It held up to 1,200 people but by the time it was demolished, in 1967, the seating capacity was 1,600. It had become a cinema and café by 1931.

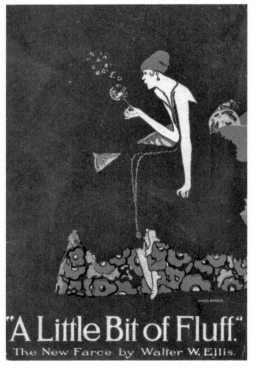

"A Little Bit of Fluff."
The New Farce by Walter W. Ellis.

This show was typical of the type of programme seen on the stage of the Theatre Royal in the 1920s, six nights a week, twice nightly at 6.40 and 8.45. This one by Walter W. Ellis was from the Criterion Theatre in London.

Demolition of the Grand Theatre on Jubilee Street in August 1951. In its heyday this was the home of variety and music hall. On the left hand side is one of a number of old playbills showing the head of the late Will Murray in the role he made famous in *Caseys Court*. His family ran the Grand until its closure. This is now the site of the post office telephone building.

The Prince's Theatre as seen on the cover of a programme from 1911 when the popular drama, *Sexton Blake*, was being performed.

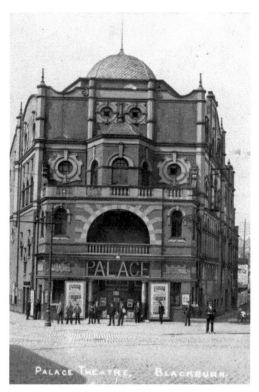

The Palace Theatre, Jubilee Street, as seen from the Boulevard in 1899. It seated over 2,000 people and was opened in December of that year. It was of two-tier construction and cost £30,000 to build. It was converted to a cinema in 1936 and was demolished in 1984, the site becoming, like that of its companion the Rialto in Penny Street, a car park.

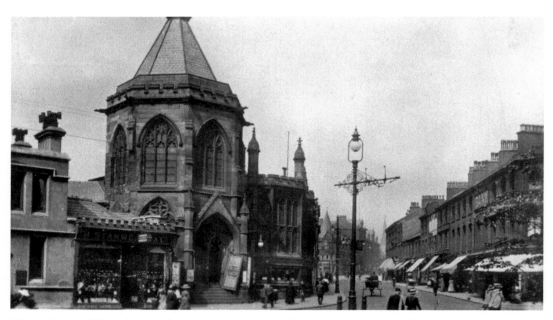

The Exchange Hall in King William Street was originally built as a Cotton Exchange and became a cinema in 1912. Originally the Majestic, it became the New Majestic then the Essoldo, the Classic, Unit Four, and last known as Apollo 5. What's in a name?

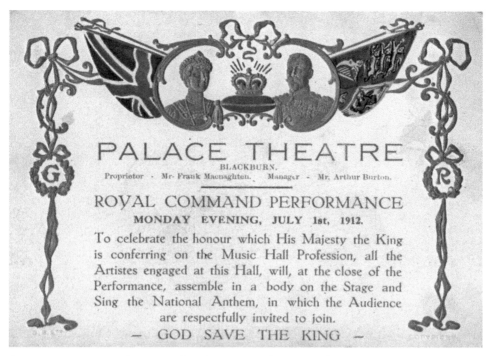

PALACE THEATRE

BLACKBURN.

Proprietor - Mr. Frank Macnaghten. Manager - Mr. Arthur Burton.

ROYAL COMMAND PERFORMANCE

MONDAY EVENING, JULY 1st, 1912.

To celebrate the honour which His Majesty the King is conferring on the Music Hall Profession, all the Artistes engaged at this Hall, will, at the close of the Performance, assemble in a body on the Stage and Sing the National Anthem, in which the Audience are respectfully invited to join.

— GOD SAVE THE KING —

An invitation to a Royal Command Performance at the Palace Theatre in 1912.

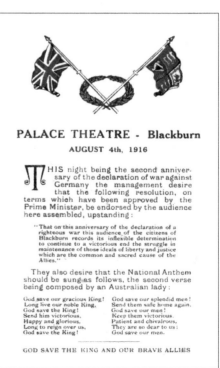

PALACE THEATRE - Blackburn

AUGUST 4th, 1916

THIS night being the second anniversary of the declaration of war against Germany the management desire that the following resolution, on terms which have been approved by the Prime Minister, be endorsed by the audience here assembled, upstanding:

"That on this anniversary of the declaration of a righteous war this audience of the citizens of Blackburn records its inflexible determination to continue to a victorious end the struggle in maintenance of those ideals of liberty and justice which are the common and sacred cause of the Allies."

They also desire that the National Anthem should be sung as follows, the second verse being composed by an Australian lady:

God save our gracious King!
Long live our noble King,
God save the King!
Send him victorious,
Happy and glorious,
Long to reign over us,
God save the King!

God save our splendid men!
Send them safe home again.
God save our men!
Keep them victorious.
Patient and chivalrous,
They are so dear to us:
God save our men.

GOD SAVE THE KING AND OUR BRAVE ALLIES

This card was issued by the Palace Theatre on 4 August 1916, the second anniversary of the declaration of war against Germany.

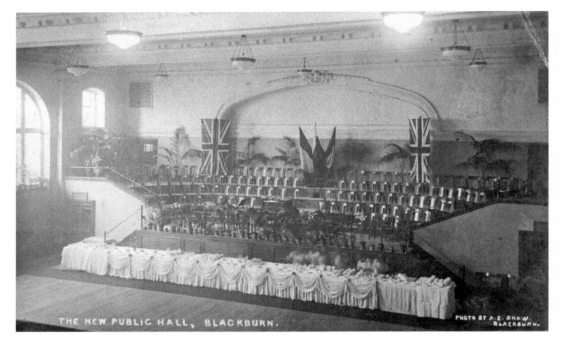

The stage and organ at King George's Hall. Designed to be the main function room of the three public halls it could accommodate 1,800 customers on the main floor and 840 on the balcony.

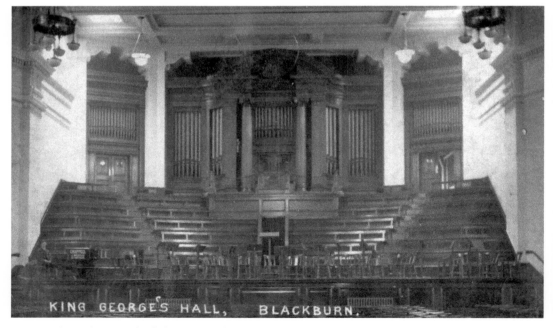

An A. E. Shaw photograph of The New Public Hall in about 1910. This one is presumably the assembly hall. The third one was the lecture hall.

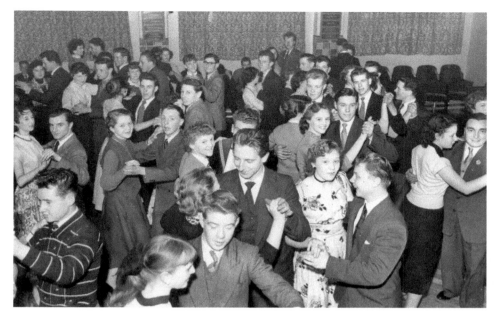

A scene at Park Gates Academy in 1956, opposite the Entrance to Corporation Park. If you wanted to learn to dance this was the place to go. No wallflowers allowed here, you had to get up and dance! The proprietor, Walter Ogden ('strictly ballroom') was born in Nelson and worked in the mills until he could afford to open his own dance school. He taught for nearly half a century and died in 1994 at the age of seventy-nine.

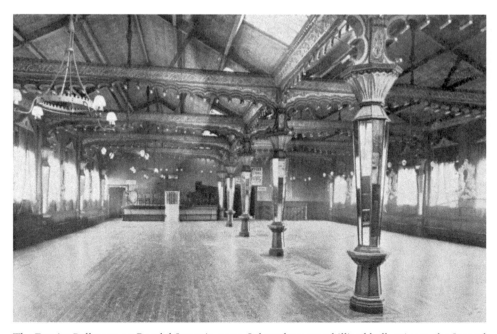

The Empire Ballroom on Randal Street in 1910. It later became a billiard hall, prior to the Second World War, and was still going strong in the 1950s.

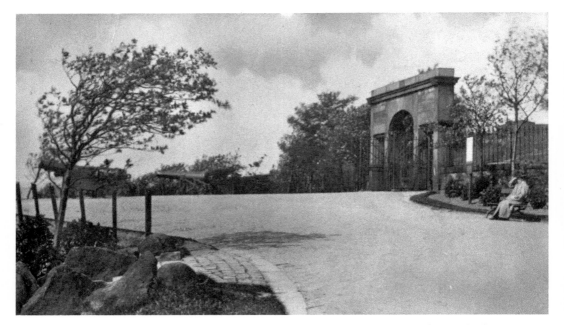

The east gate of Queen's Park in 1922 with guns from the Crimean War in the background. The gate has now been demolished but some of the stones have been left on the ground to prevent vehicle access. The guns, like those that were at Corporation Park, may have been taken for scrap during the Second World War.

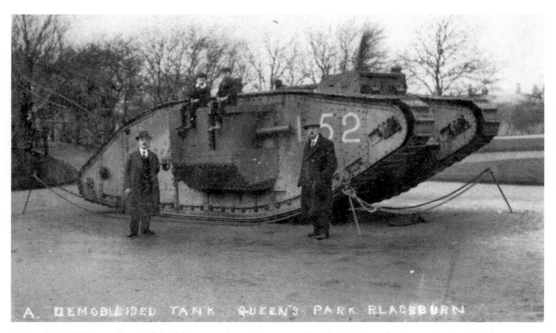

A. DEMOBILISED TANK QUEEN'S PARK BLACKBURN

A First World War tank which had been used to raise money for the War Bonds Campaign in Blackburn run by the National War Savings Committee. Their slogan was 'Feed the guns with War Bonds'. Was this its final resting place and were these men local dignitaries?

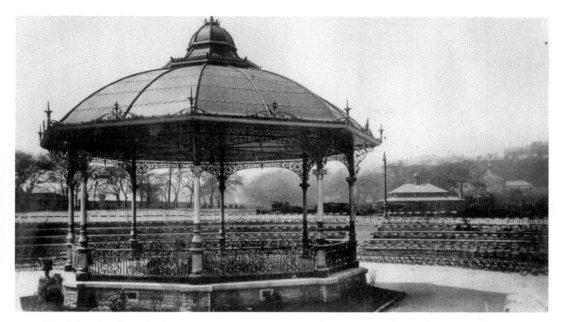

The New Bandstand of 1909 seen in Corporation Park on West Park Road opposite the Grammar School in 1911. The Open Air School is in the background. This stand replaced another which stood from 1880 to 1908. It was opened on 17 September by Cllr J.H. Higginson, attended by 6,000 people. An audience of 1,200 could be seated on collapsible iron chairs at a cost of one penny a time. The opening performance was given by the band of the Border Regiment who played Lehar's *The Merry Widow* and a selection of Harry Lauder's songs.

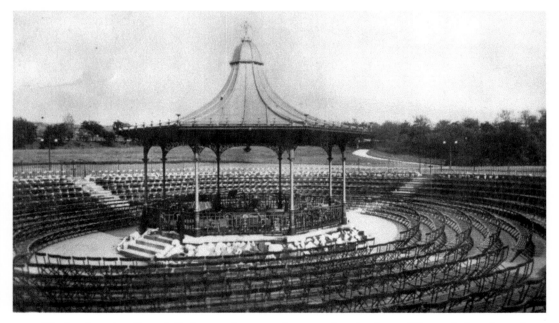

The bandstand at Queen's Park – another extensive area of seating but a different design of stand.

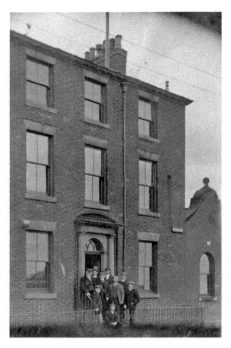

The Witton Club, Redlam, on the corner of Preston Old Road and Spring Lane. Peter Haslam, on the left of the group, was over eighty years of age at the time of the photograph in 1917. Bob Hamer is the only bareheaded man in the group. This building was recently demolished to widen the pavement for pedestrians.

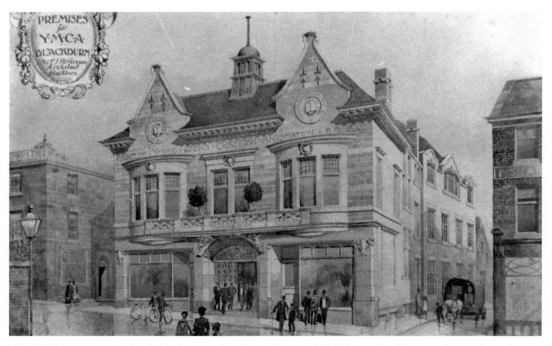

The YMCA premises in Limbrick designed by F.J. Parkinson of Blackburn. Lord Kinnaird, President of the National Council of the YMCA, laid the foundation stone for the new building on 9 May 1908 and it was officially opened by Cllr Scholes on 21 July 1910. The Sir Charles Napier public house opened here when the YMCA moved into new purpose built premises in Clarence Street.

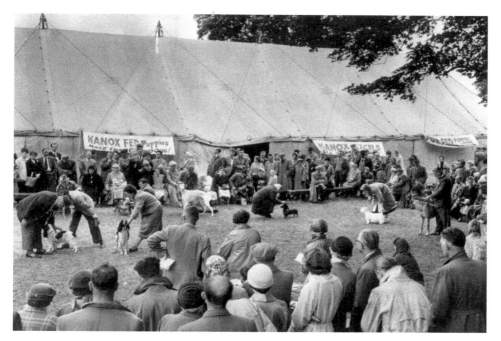

Blackburn Show at Witton Park in 1958. Judges inspect a class for pet dogs. Agricultural Shows had been held, on and off, from 1881.

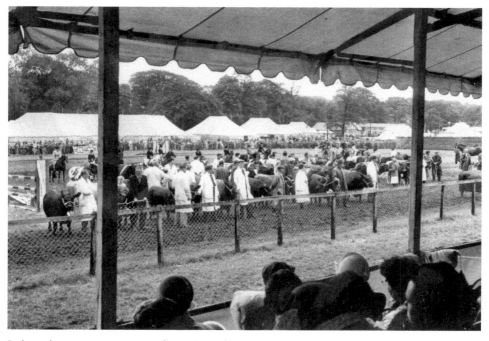

Judges about to present prizes for a class of bulls with horse riders ready in the background to take part in a jumping event.

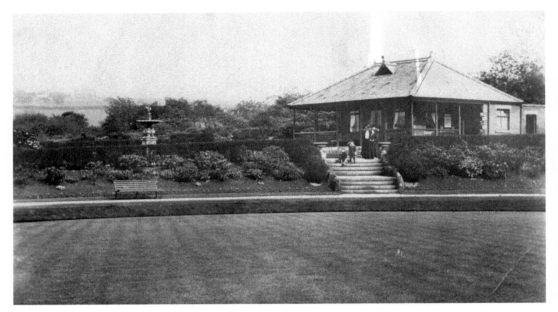

One of four bowling greens still in use in Queen's Park showing the ornate fountain in the background, opened on 20 June 1887. The pavilion cannot be seen now because of the height and density of the bushes.

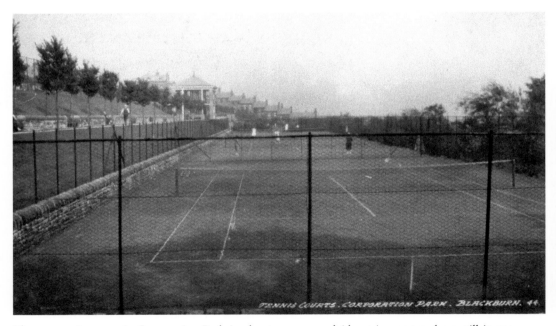

The ten tennis courts in Corporation Park in about 1939 were laid out in 1924 and are still in use. These are accessed from Revidge Road.

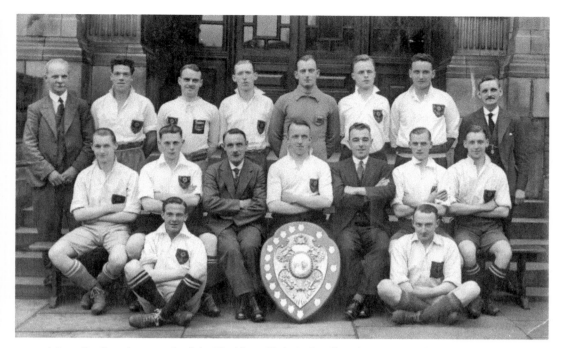

A Jetta Studios photograph of the Blackburn Technical College Amateur Football Club team who were winners of the Lancashire Amateur Shield in the 1929/30 season. Their main local rivals were the Old Blackburnians.

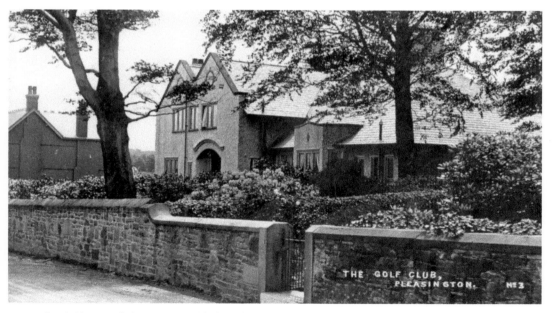

The clubhouse of Pleasington Golf Club photographed in 1920. It was opened on 9 June 1910 and, with slight alterations, remained as seen here until Jack Walker opened the new clubhouse – a development costing £1m – on 14 September 1997.

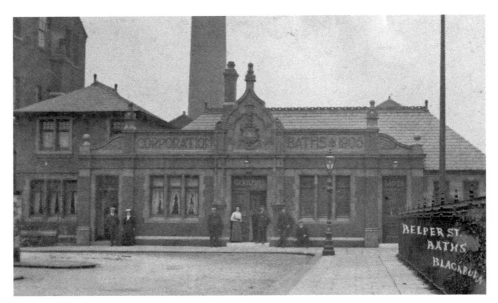

The Belper Street baths were built in 1905 at a cost of £9,328. In addition to the plunge bath, which was 75 ft long and 30 ft wide with a depth of 3 ft to 6 ft 6 in, there were forty-seven dressing boxes, one children's dressing room, slipper baths (seventeen male, fourteen female), and a Russian bath comprising hot room, shower room, cooling room, and sixteen dressing boxes. These baths were in addition to the two baths at Freckleton Street and another being built at this time under the school at Blakey Moor.

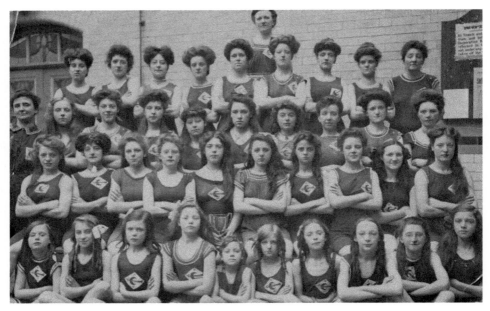

The Blackburn Clarion Swimming Club, Ladies' Section, photographed in 1908. On the reverse of this postcard it says that Polly Hobkirk is holding the National Cup for winning the 100 yds. Unfortunately the ASA was unable to confirm this when I checked with them.

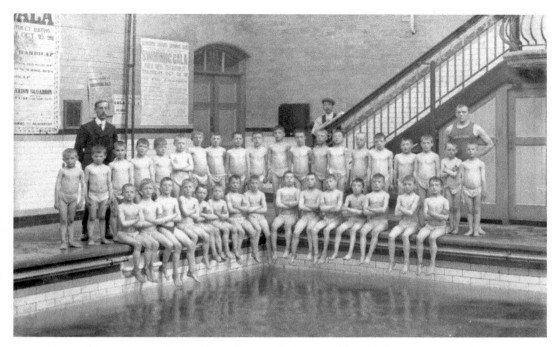

A class of boy swimmers in Freckleton Street baths in 1908. Most of them are wearing the trunks which were provided for hire. The popularity of swimming at the time can be seen by the number of posters on the wall advertising galas which were being held.

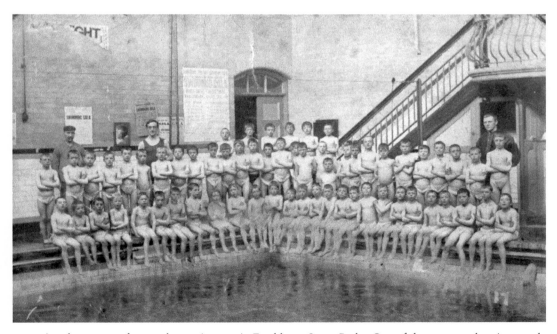

Another group of young boy swimmers in Freckleton Street Baths. One of the posters advertises a gala at Longsight in Manchester.

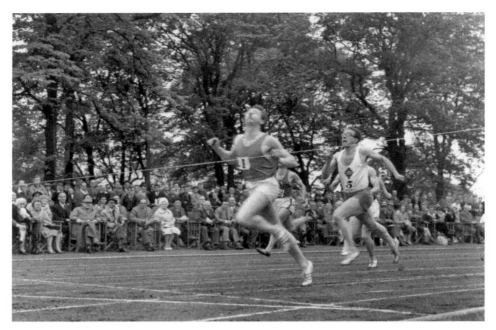

A Witton Park Athletics Meeting in 1972. The event is being watched by Ald. Eddie and other officials and shows a 100 yds senior semi-final race being won by A. Meakin (9.8 secs) with D. Hermann, second (9.9 secs) and T. Dennis, third (10.1 secs).

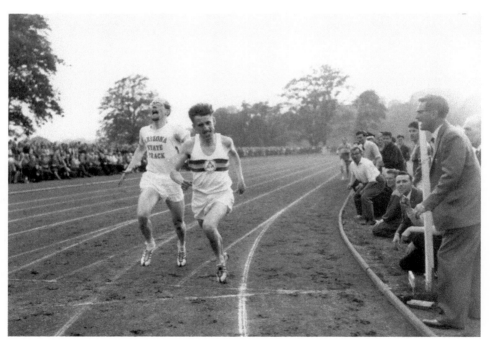

This photograph shows the Yorkshireman Derek Ibbotson, apparently, winning the one mile race. Wearing his AAA vest, Derek had been the British mile record holder.

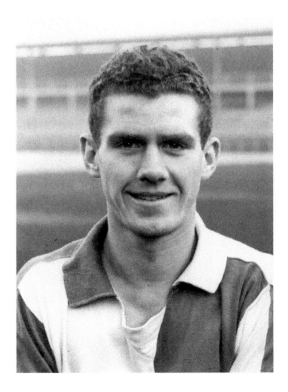

Generally acknowledged to be the two favourite Blackburn Rovers stars of the modern era: Ronnie Clayton (top) and Bryan Douglas. Both are still ardent Rovers' fans today. Ronnie, a Prestonian by birth, came to the Rovers at the age of fourteen while Dougie was born and bred in Blackburn. Ronnie earned thirty-five caps playing with England and was captain five times. Dougie earned thirty-six caps.

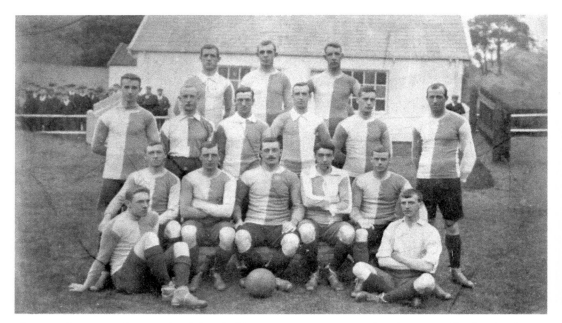

This 1904/5 season photograph of the Blackburn Rovers team was taken by J. Frankland, a local photographer, and published as a postcard by J. Neville of Darwen Street. The Rovers finished thirteenth in Division 1.

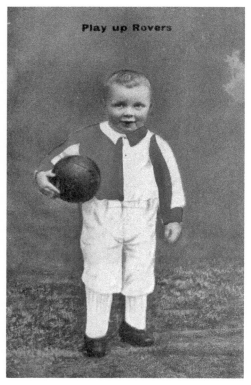

A 1909 Rovers supporter showing the strip of the time. Do you remember the leather ball?

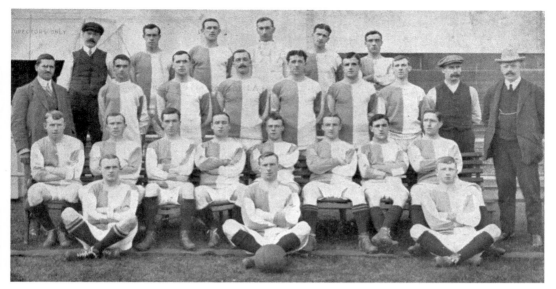

This photograph by R. Scott & Co. was taken of the Rovers somewhere between 1907-1915.

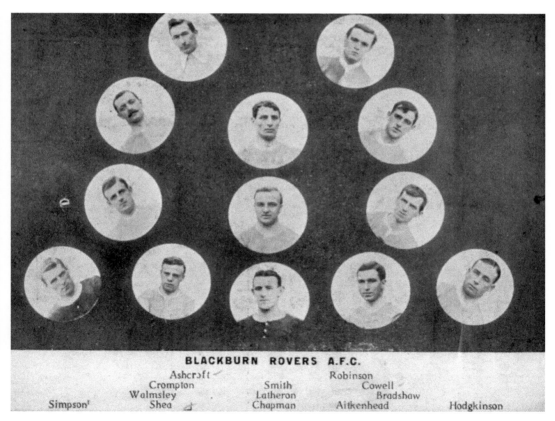

BLACKBURN ROVERS A.F.C.

	Ashcroft		Robinson	
	Crompton	Smith	Cowell	
	Walmsley	Latheron	Bradshaw	
Simpson	Shea	Chapman	Aitkenhead	Hodgkinson

A montage of individual Rovers player's photographs which is not dated but is between 1913 and 1920.

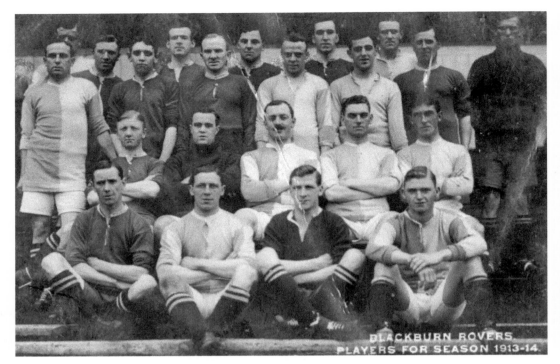

The Rovers, captained by Bob Crompton, were League Division 1 Champions in 1913/14. Left to right, back row: A. Walmsley, D. Shea, H. McGrory, J. Johnston, W. Aitkenhead, G. Chapman, H. Langtree. Middle row: W. Anthony, T. Jaques, T. Suttie, J. Orr, A. Cowell, J. Simpson. Seated: E. Latheron, A. Robinson, R. Crompton, A. Bell, A. McGhie. Front row: J. Hodgkinson, J. Clennel, G. Porteous, W. Goodwin.

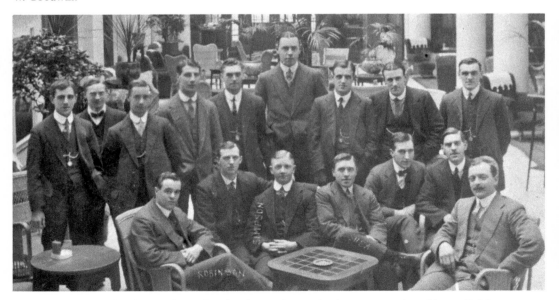

The champions at Cleveleys Hydro in less familiar garb. On the front row at the table are Robinson, Simpson and Shea.

seven

Transport

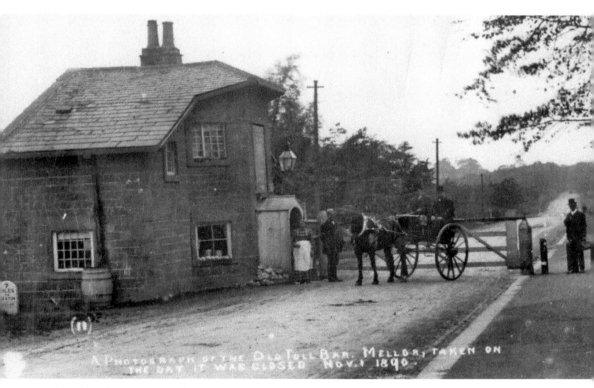

The Old Toll Bar opposite the Yew Tree public house, now the County Hotel, in 1910. It opened its gates, or took down its bar, to become toll free on 2 November 1890.

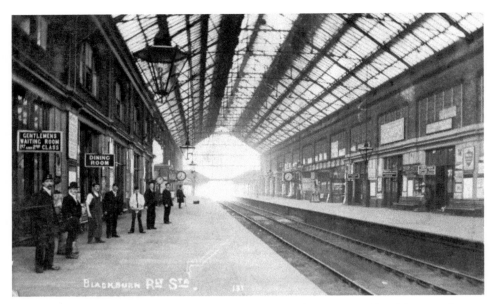

Blackburn railway station photographed by Shaw & Son of Preston New Road, in around 1910. The two large clocks visible in this picture have now been removed during current redevelopment and will be restored and returned to the new station on its completion. The first line was opened between Blackburn and Preston on Whit Monday 1846, followed by connections to Bolton and Chatburn in 1850. Next were Wigan and Chorley on 1 December 1869 and then the loop-line to Padiham and Rosegrove was opened for traffic on 1 June 1877. The present station was opened in 1886 and cost £100,000.

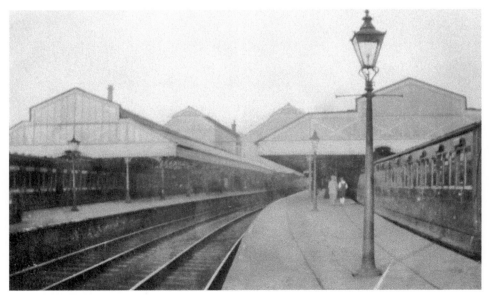

A view of the main platforms from the Darwen Street end which were extensively used for the mass exodus of holiday makers in wakes fortnight.

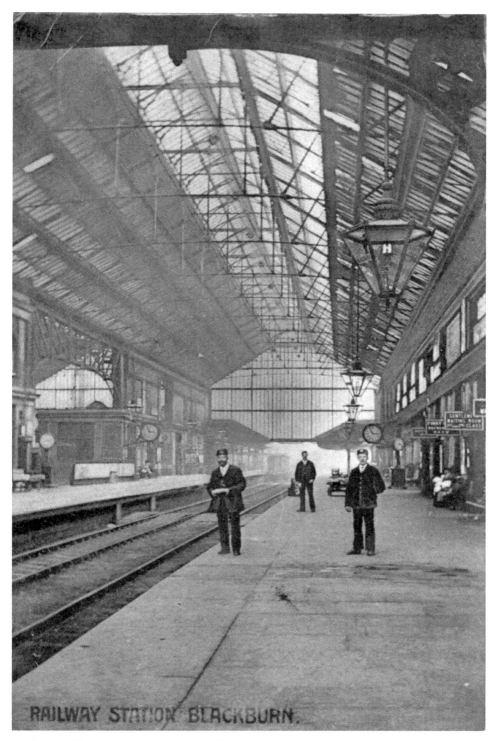

RAILWAY STATION BLACKBURN.

Platform staff await the arrival of a train in 1908.

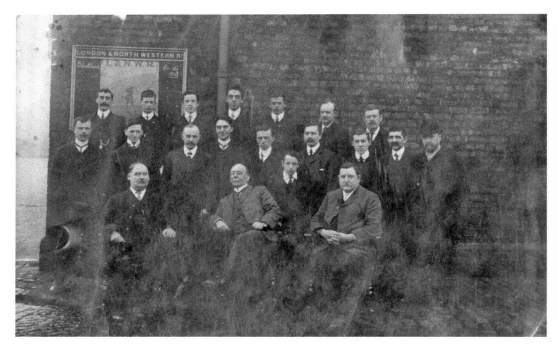

A formal group photograph of the Blackburn staff of the London & North Western Railway based in Galligreaves Street, 1910. Robert Bell was the agent in 1915.

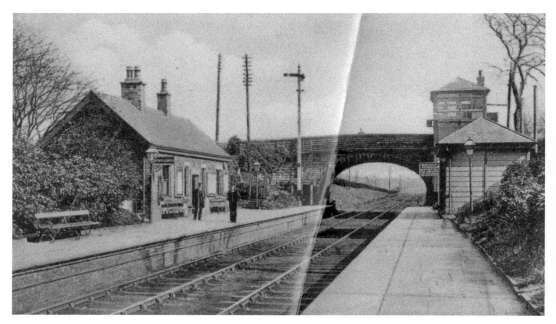

Pleasington railway station, looking towards Blackburn, in 1908.

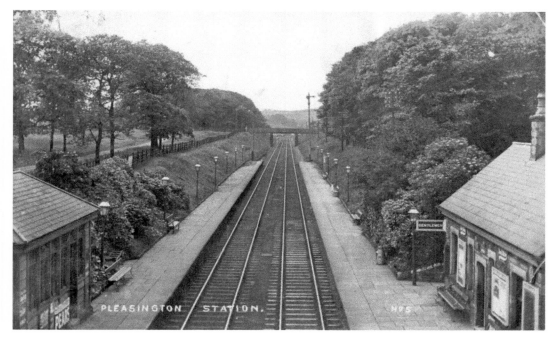

Pleasington station, with the golf links on the left and Hoghton ahead, photographed by Shaw.

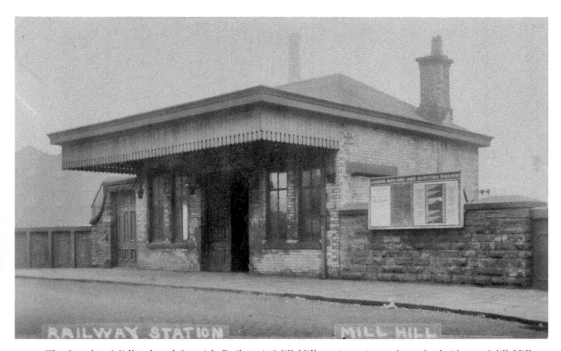

The London Midland and Scottish Railway's Mill Hill station, situated on the bridge at Mill Hill, as it was in 1915. This station was opened in 1884 to accommodate the increasing population but was demolished in Beechings railway cuts of the 1960s. The photograph was by Burton and Garland.

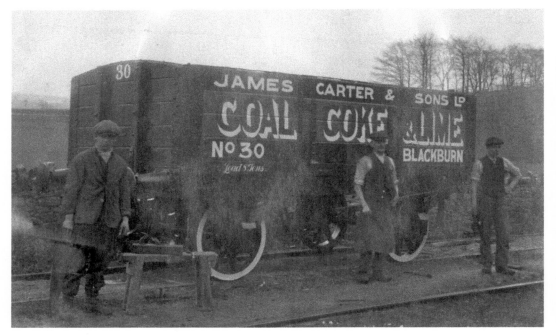

A typical rail truck of the steam era. James Carter & Sons Ltd transported lime from Clitheroe and returned with coal and coke for the Ribble Valley to the Clitheroe sidings.

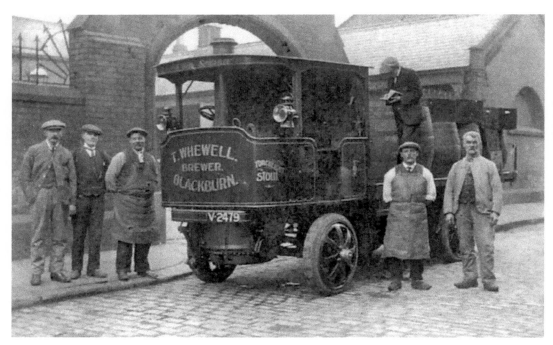

A pre-1914 Sentinel steam wagon from Whewell's Victoria Brewery on Adelaide Street and George St West. The brewery was taken over by Blackburn Brewery and ultimately by Dutton's.

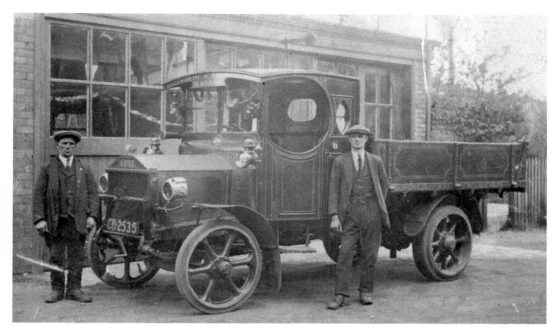

A Napier flat wagon registered before 1910 and owned by Duckworth & Eddleston of Roe Lee Mills.

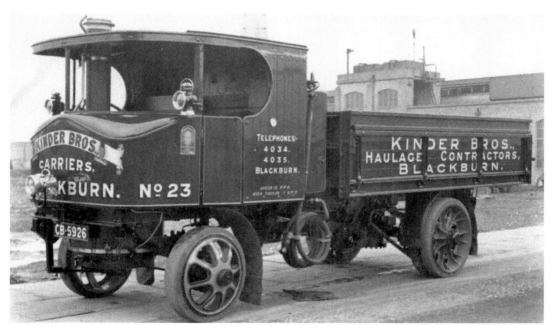

A brand new Sentinel steam wagon photographed outside the Shrewsbury works, c. 1915. This appears to be the twenty-third vehicle to be purchased by Kinder Bros., haulage contractors, of Blackburn. The firm was based on Canterbury Street and proudly advertised that they 'carried goods by steam motor to all parts of Lancashire'. Its top speed was 12 mph and 5 mph with trailer.

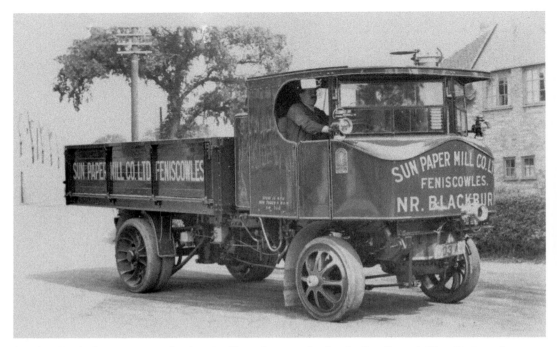

Another Sentinel steam wagon leaving the Shrewsbury works for the Sun Paper Mill at Feniscowles, *c.* 1915. This was a faster model than the previous one, being able to do 16 mph and 8 mph with a trailer!

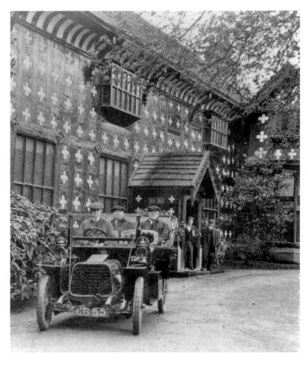

A Blackburn registered 1904 open tourer on a visit to Samlesbury Hall with some distinguished-looking Blackburn gentlemen on board.

eight

The Lighter Side

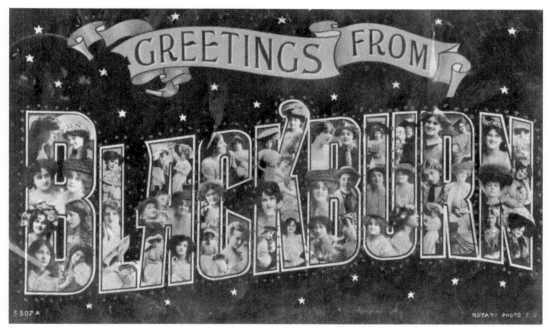

A glossy, coloured greetings card of 1909 published by Rotary of London and similar to ones still available today.

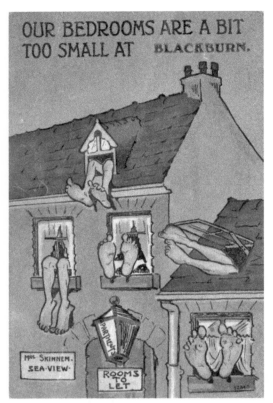

Blackpool wasn't the only town to have comic postcards but it still sold them long after the trade had died elsewhere. I don't know where the sea-view is!

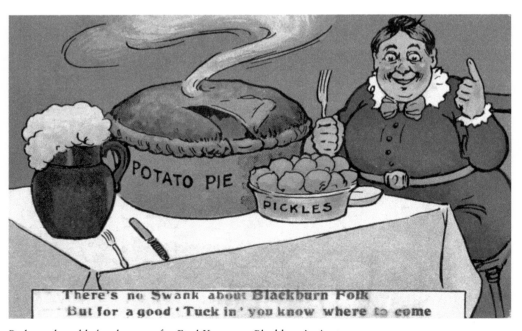

Perhaps the table has been set for Fred Kempster, Blackburn's giant.

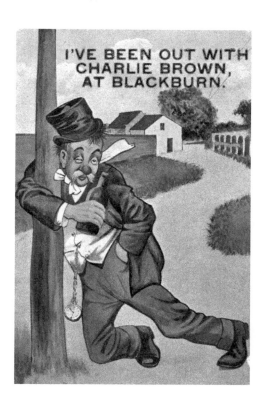

He must have had too much Nuttall's Brown Ale!

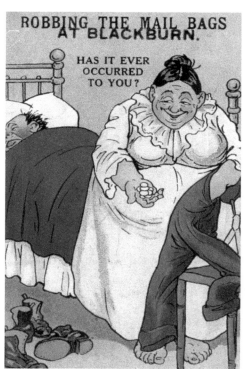

A common occurrence if my mother's stories are to be believed.

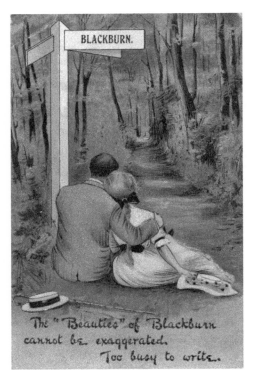

I've not seen any signposts in Billinge Woods.

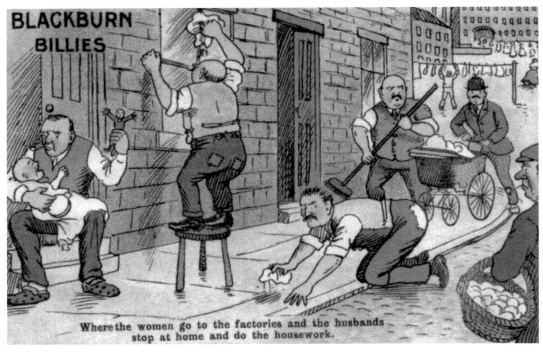

I thought this was a new idea?

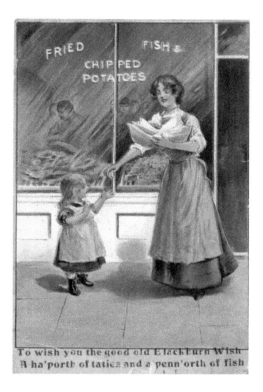

The original Blackburn take-away.

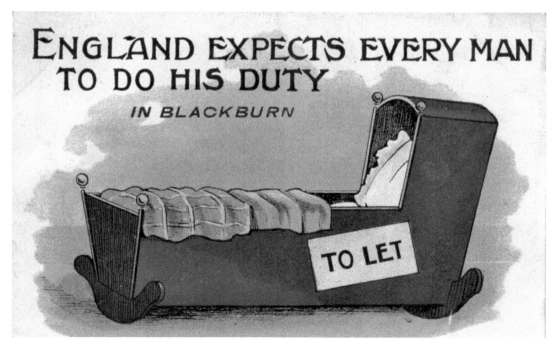

What an invitation!

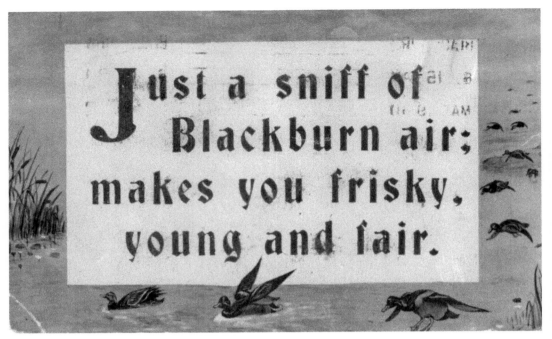

Most of the postcard messages I've seen sent from Blackburn mention the rain.

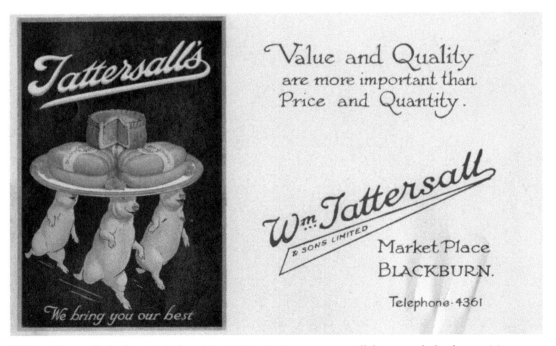

William Tattersall & Sons Ltd, based in St Peter's Street, were well known wholesale provision merchants. They were also canners and supplied the armed forces.

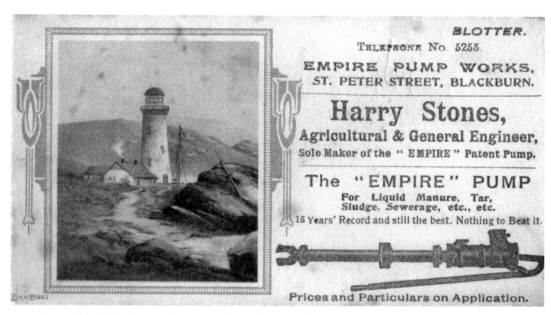

A very handy implement for putting the tar between the sets or cobbles.

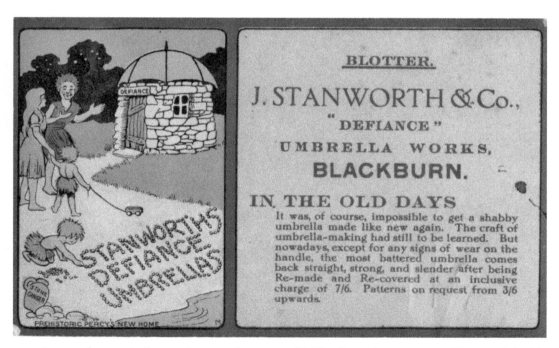

Stanworths were in Darwen Street, at the corner of Jubilee Street, for many years. They specialised in umbrellas and luggage.

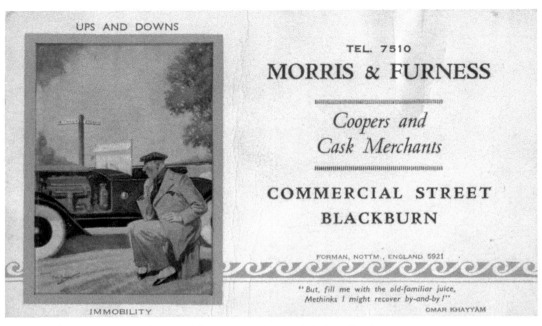

Morris and Furness were at Commercial Street which was off Bolton Road.

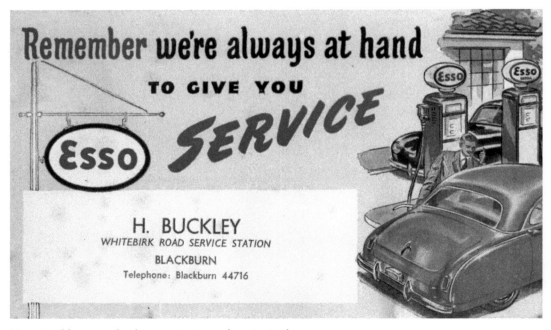

Harry Buckley was a haulage contractor and carrier in the 1950s.

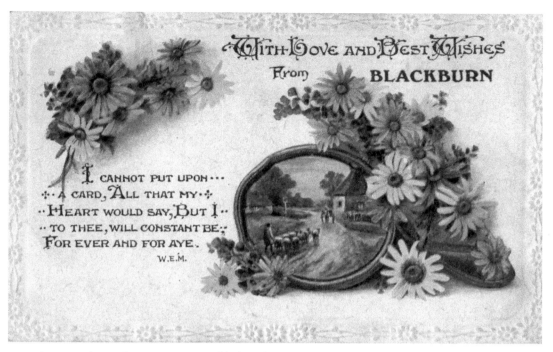

With Love and Best Wishes
From
BLACKBURN

I CANNOT PUT UPON···
··A CARD, ALL THAT MY·
··HEART WOULD SAY, BUT I··
··TO THEE, WILL CONSTANT BE··
FOR EVER AND FOR AYE.
W.E.M.

A postcard served as a greetings card before the First World War.

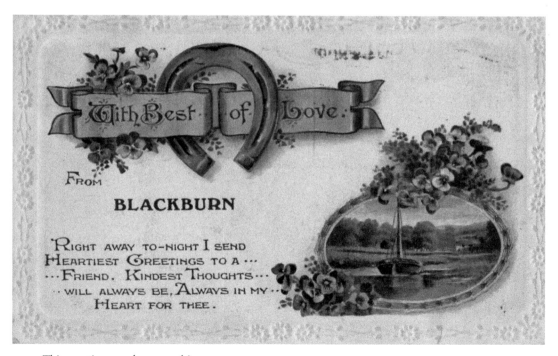

With Best of Love.
FROM
BLACKBURN

RIGHT AWAY TO-NIGHT I SEND
HEARTIEST GREETINGS TO A···
···FRIEND. KINDEST THOUGHTS···
··WILL ALWAYS BE, ALWAYS IN MY···
HEART FOR THEE.

This greetings card was used in 1913.

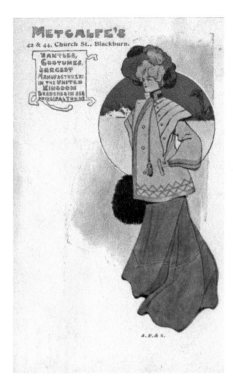

Fashion wasn't the monopoly of London. Cards like these were sent everywhere between the wars. One wonders if the claim, 'largest manufacturer in the United Kingdom' could really be true.

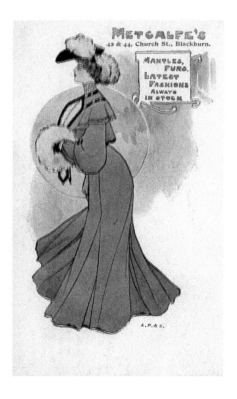